I Have Learned from the Least

I Have Learned *from the* Least

My Life, My Hopes

Cardinal Luis Antonio Tagle

**Edited by Gerolamo Fazzini
and Lorenzo Fazzini**

Translated by Dinah Livingstone

ORBIS BOOKS
Maryknoll, New York 10545

ORBIS BOOKS
Maryknoll, New York 10545

Fathers and Brothers
MARYKNOLL™
TOGETHER IN GOD'S MISSION OF MERCY

Founded in 1970, Orbis Books endeavors to publish works that enlighten the mind, nourish the spirit, and challenge the conscience. The publishing arm of the Maryknoll Fathers and Brothers, Orbis seeks to explore the global dimensions of the Christian faith and mission, to invite dialogue with diverse cultures and religious traditions, and to serve the cause of reconciliation and peace. The books published reflect the views of their authors and do not represent the official position of the Maryknoll Society. To learn more about Maryknoll and Orbis Books, please visit our website at www.maryknollsociety.org.

Library of Congress Cataloging-in-Publication Data

Names: Tagle, Luis Antonio, author. | Fazzini, Gerolamo, 1962- editor.
Title: I have learned from the least : my life, my hopes / Cardinal Luis
    Antonio Tagle ; edited by Gerolamo Fazzini and Lorenzo Fazzini ;
    translated by Dinah Livingstone.
Other titles: Ho imparato dagli ultimi. English
Description: Maryknoll : Orbis Books, 2017.
Identifiers: LCCN 2017002621 (print) | LCCN 2017019895 (ebook) |
    ISBN 9781608337064 (e-book) | ISBN 9781626982413 (pbk.)
Subjects: LCSH: Tagle, Luis Antonio. | Cardinals—Philippines—
    Biography.
Classification: LCC BX4705.T237 (ebook) | LCC BX4705.T237 A3 2017
    (print) | DDC 282.092 [B]—dc23
LC record available at https://lccn.loc.gov/2017002621

Contents

Introduction

"During the next few days my former theology teacher will be in Rome. He is called Antonio Tagle. Now he is bishop of a city near Manila. It would be interesting to interview him." It was in 2005 when Fabio Motta, a missionary from the Pontifical Institute for Foreign Missions, then stationed in the Philippines, suggested this to the monthly magazine *Mondo e Missione.* Tagle had arrived in Rome to take part in the Synod on the Eucharist. It was a pleasant surprise to receive a prompt and positive reply from him, the youngest bishop attending the synod (he was forty-eight). The interview, published in November 2005, revealed a surprising man, who combined theological depth with extraordinary pastoral sensitivity.

Second flash. In October 2012 we were in the midst of the scandals that beset the Catholic Church during Benedict XVI's papacy—Vatileaks, the Vatican Bank scandal, clergy sex abuse. The fathers of the Pontifical Institute for Foreign Missions told the publisher EMI (Editrice Missionaria Italiana) about a book published by Tagle, who at that time was archbishop of Manila and had just been made a cardinal by Pope Benedict.

"Here's his mobile number, contact him. You'll see that he'll be very willing to help," said Father Piero Masolo, who was also an ex-student of Tagle. No sooner said than done. A few days before he was invested as cardinal, Tagle made himself available for an interview and agreed for us to publish *Easter People*,[1] his first book translated into Italian. The conversation was intended to last for just half an hour but went on for several hours. When it was over, we had a clear feeling: we had met a genuine pastor, simple and passionate, who suggested the church needed a "bath of humility" as the only way to become credible to the world.

With the 2013 conclave, which resulted in the election of Pope Francis, Tagle became known worldwide. His name appeared in many newspapers in the "Toto-Papa" (pope betting) that followed Benedict XVI's unexpected resignation. Public opinion, and of course not just Italian, began to know the face and (human and spiritual) profile of the "Filipino Cardinal." For some time the most attentive observers had already grasped his personal stature, solid learning, and pastoral passion. As Enzo Bianchi, prior of the Bose Community, said of him: "Tagle is a man of the gospel who really knows how to talk about Jesus Christ." "He has the charisma of John Paul II and the theological stature of Benedict XVI," declared the *Los Angeles Times*. "Tagle has the mind of a theologian, the soul of a musician, and the heart of a pastor," said John

---

1. *Easter People: Living Community* was published by Orbis Books in 2005. Italian translation: *Gente di Pasqua* (Milan: EMI, 2013).

Allen, number one Vatican expert in the United States. In the run up to the 2013 conclave the *Corriere della Sera* defined him more soberly as "an emergent personality of the Eastern church," while *Repubblica* pointed out "his two sides: sophisticated theologian and a pastor who cares about the lives of the poor."

When the media circus of the conclave was over, a question still remained: who really is Tagle? Why does he make such a strong impression, especially when he is heard for the first time? Where does this cardinal come from, who often wore "civilian clothes," and who didn't even have a car when he was a bishop? ("I preferred to go by bus, so as to meet people.") Who was this prince of the church who did not love the great pomp typical of so many church dignitaries? Many—including his American mentor, Father Joseph A. Komonchak—consider him to be one of the most brilliant and able theologians of recent years. This curiosity gave rise to the desire to question the man himself directly. Tagle's own reluctance had to be overcome; he did not want to talk about himself except in terms of faith and gratitude. So the idea was born of this autobiography in the form of a dialogue.

Until a few years ago Luis Antonio Gokim Tagle (Gokim is his Chinese mother's surname) was known in the West almost exclusively within the restricted circle of theologians. He contributed to the monumental *History of Vatican II* [2] edited by Giuseppe Alberigo (and Joseph A.

2. Italian edition in five volumes, *Storia del Concilio Vaticano*

Komonchak, for the English edition). Years before that he took part in Bologna in the meetings of the Foundation for Religious Sciences between scholars and historians from all over Europe and beyond. Since 1997 he has been a member of the International Theological Commission in Rome, which was convoked by the then-Cardinal Josef Ratzinger, prefect of the Congregation for the Doctrine of the Faith and the Commission's president.

During the years that followed, Tagle became increasingly involved in Vatican organizations: in 1998 he was appointed as an "expert" at the Synod on Asia; in 2005 he was the Filipino delegate for the Synod on the Eucharist; likewise in 2008 for the Synod on the Word of God. In the two most recent cases the assembly of bishops from all over the world elected him to the postsynodal council, the group that drew up the synthesis of their work. In 2012, at the Synod on the New Preaching of the Gospel (Evangelization), Tagle was nominated vice-president of the Commission for the final message. In this case too the assembly elected him to the postsynodal council. Pope Francis wanted him as president of the 2014 and 2015 synods, both of which were on the subject of the family.

II, edited by Giuseppe Alberigo (Bologna: Il Mulino,1995–2001). New updated, expanded edition, edited by Alberto Melloni, (Louvain: Peeters/Bologna: Il Mulino, 2012–2015). English editions: *History of Vatican II*, ed. Giuseppe Alberigo and Joseph Komonchak, 5 vols. (Louvain: Peeters/Maryknoll, NY: Orbis Books, 1995–2006).

Pope Francis has given him many jobs: member of the Congregation for Catholic Education, member of the pontifical councils for the family (he is a member of the presidential committee), for migrants, for the laity. Finally, in 2015, he was elected as president of Caritas Internationalis and of the Catholic Biblical Federation.

This book is the result of a dozen or so meetings and long interviews, which took place either in Rome at the Filipino College, or in Tagle's residence in the Philippines, in Intramuros, the "ancient heart" of Manila, which is like a treasure chest of street names and buildings that go back to the period when the most Catholic country in Asia was a Spanish colony. There we were able to have lunch with him and his "family" (which also includes a disabled person) in plain and simple style.

We put many questions to Tagle in long, far-reaching conversations. He then reviewed, re-read, corrected, and completed the whole manuscript. He set aside the time to do this amid countless other national and international commitments. Thus the editors can bear witness that the author of this book is truly the cardinal, speaking here about himself and humbly and frankly presenting his own vision of the world, his faith, and his life. We have also followed him and seen him at work on several occasions, both in Italy and in Manila. We then approached a good number of people who have had (or still have) Tagle as their pastor.

In our conversation with the cardinal we have gone

back step by step over his life and the choices he has made. Meanwhile at every stage of his human, spiritual, and ecclesial development, the conversation extended to talking about the context in which the gospel is called to become history today. So this is an autobiography, but one in which our author also speaks about "hot" topics concerning faith, the church, the challenges of the world and society.

In conclusion: During the preparation of this book we have seen many instances of the care taken by the cardinal, especially in the attention he pays to individual people. Working on this book has been an extraordinary human experience, a journey taken in the company of someone who, especially in recent times as Vatican and international duties have mounted, has seen his life overwhelmed with duties and demands. Nevertheless, he never lost his good humor and his ability to put problems into perspective with one of his proverbial laughs or an enjoyable anecdote. At Rimini during the 2014 Franciscan Festival he told an unforgettable one: "At the end of my lecture at the Eucharistic Congress in Quebec, in 2008, a cardinal came up to me: 'Excellency, thank you for your speech,' he said. 'May I ask you to give me the text? I would really enjoy reading it over. I am the archbishop of Buenos Aires, Jorge Maria Bergoglio.' Of course I gave it to him. What a surprise when from Buenos Aires he began to write personal letters to me in Imus, where I was bishop. I never answered him for lack of time. Think how valuable those letters would be today!" And he burst out laughing to play down the admiration that the future pope showed for the young Bishop Tagle.

And in our conversations too there was no lack of smiles and jokes from Cardinal Chito (his family nickname, an abbreviation of the diminutive Luisito). These smiles quite often disconcerted his questioner, at a loss to understand how Tagle found the gusto to be ironical and "light," when he had so many things on his mind and was beset by problems that would stress most of us out. We hope the reader will feel the same astonishment that we did, and feel how the surprising serenity and joyfulness that this man constantly displays have deep roots that draw their strength from above.

Gerolamo and Lorenzo Fazzini

Son of the People

"Whenever a Swiss guard in the Vatican calls me 'Your Eminence' I always feel amazed. Me a cardinal? To myself I am always Gokim Tagle, a simple priest called by the Lord to serve."

This isn't the false modesty of the "baby cardinal" Tagle (for some years he has been the second youngest cardinal in the Sacred College). It really is a natural attitude of Bishop Chito (his familiar nickname, which he himself uses on his Twitter account). He makes himself available to others with great simplicity, without any formality. His style is rooted in his personal history, a man who grew up in a working-class family that was very simple and deeply religious.

Today Cardinal Tagle is a person of international standing; he leads one of the world's most populous cities; he is a theologian with a worldwide reputation (having studied in the United States as well as in Italy) and has received degrees and honorary doctorates from all over the world. As a conference speaker he is in demand, from the Davos Forum to the Synod of Bishops, and appreciated in a number of countries. But from his childhood he grew up in an environment deeply imbued with *the simple faith of the people, consisting of traditional prayers and devotion to the Madonna. This remains crucial to his history and has also left its mark on his pastoral style. We cannot understand Tagle's personality if we do not start with his family and cultural roots, closely connected with his Filipino identity, firmly set in popular Christianity and a strong sense of family and home.*

Today many people consider Tagle to be one of the cardinals closest to the style and teaching of Pope Francis (Jorge Bergoglio), as can be seen from the many responsibilities Pope Francis has given him. It is no surprise that this should happen. Both in his way of behaving and of speaking we find the same simplicity and friendliness in his relations with people that we have learned to appreciate in the Argentinian pope.

Tell us something about your parents and family.

My mother's family came from the region of Dagupan, in the province of Pangasinan, in the northern part of the island of Luzon. My mother, Milagros Gokim, is of Chinese descent. As a child her father came from China with an uncle on business, but then remained in the Philippines. He got married here and then did not return to China. My maternal grandmother was also of mixed Filipino–Chinese blood.

My mother was one of nine children. My grandfather worked for a cigar company. My grandmother looked after the house. They were great workers. My father's family came from Imus, a little city in the province of Cavite, situated twenty-five kilometers south of Manila. My father, Manuel Senior, lost his father as a child; he died during the Japanese occupation when a bomb exploded. My father himself was wounded. Today he still has some fragments of that device in his body. My paternal grandmother kept my father's family going with five children, that is, four daughters and one son, my father. She worked as a cook in a restaurant with her sister. My grandmother worked very hard as she was the single parent. She was often absent from family meals because of her work in the restaurant. Later she got a stomach tumor which led to her death at the age of sixty-nine.

Dad and Mom were normal, simple people: they both worked in a bank, the Equitable Bank, where they met at work. They got married on August 26, 1956. I was born a year later, on June 21, 1957, in a Manila hospital. But as a family we always lived in Imus. A year after me my sister, Irma, was born, but died a few minutes after birth. My brother, Manuel Junior, was born in 1962. For some years now he has been living in the United States. After him my mother had a fourth pregnancy, but she miscarried.

As was customary in many Filipino families at that time, my father's family lived in the same house as us: my paternal great grandfather, who died at the age of ninety-three, my paternal grandmother, my father's brothers (only his eldest sister had married and had three children), and five cousins. Living all together we learned how to be disciplined in our use of time and space, how to share things and put ourselves out for the good of all.

Do you think you still have any "Chinese" in you from your family origins and history?

I think some Chinese characteristics have passed on to me, even though my grandfather spent most of his life in the Philippines. I remember certain practices he observed, such as honoring his mother by offering her food, putting it in front of her photograph, with a few sticks of incense, or setting off fireworks to welcome the New Year, or offering a lot of food during family meals. According to Chinese custom you can and must control your expenses on other things but not on food! As well as these habits from our Chinese grandfather we learned respect for the old and family loyalty, living simply while focusing on the essential, the value of education, and work done in an ethical way based on right motivation, diligence and trust. When I was nine, my grandfather asked me to learn Chinese, since none of his grandchildren could speak it. For a whole summer I went to private lessons given by a Chinese lady, learning both Mandarin and Fukien. My fellow students were younger than me, so I was ahead of them in the lessons. But I had no opportunity to practice Chinese at home or in normal school lessons. So I stopped going to the private lessons. Now I regret not having continued learning the Chinese language.

Where did you go to school?

My parents sent me to study at a school run by Scheut Missionaries, who were from Belgium. They were members of the Congregation of the Immaculate Heart of Mary in the city of Parañaque, about fifteen kilometers away from our house. They were very simple priests with a genuinely humble lifestyle. They concentrated on what was important in the Christian education of young people. They did not want us to spend a lot of money; they told us to save money for our families. So we did not buy school books but were lent them free by the school. Each student had to take care of their books because we had to give them back at the end. Those who had looked after them carefully did not have to pay for them. This attitude taught to me by the Scheut fathers has been very useful to me for understanding the meaning of "looking after." That includes the ecological realm. Humanity has been entrusted with something not our own but which we must pass on as a legacy to others.

In the Belgian fathers we students saw so much simplicity, poverty in practice, attention to the poor, and a clear vision of the priorities in life. We were not allowed distractions; we became accustomed to looking straight at the road in front of us. I remember one Belgian missionary in particular: I am speaking about Father Paul Foulon, my teacher and also head of the school. He was very strict, but also a wise man. When we were small we were afraid of him; even his shadow struck us with dread. However, when we grew older we realized how much he loved his students. Now he has retired to Belgium, but we are still in contact.

Which of the teachings you received as a child from your parents do you consider to be the most important still today?

My grandparents and parents instilled a spirit of devotion to duty in me and taught me to work hard: "When you do something, do it well," was one of their mottoes. Another teaching I well remember from them is this: "Be a good neighbor to others. And when people ask for something from you, if you can help them, do!" But above all, my parents taught me the faith. They suffered a great deal during the war. As I have said, my paternal grandfather died from a bomb explosion during the war in 1944. He left my mother to take care of my father and his four sisters. My father, who was fourteen years old at the time, received a lasting injury. And my grandmother worked very hard in a small restaurant owned by her sister in order to be able to send her children to school. My mother's family moved elsewhere seeking a more secure job: in fact her father, being Chinese, was not well regarded by the Japanese authorities of the time. Nevertheless—thanks to their faith in God and mutual help—they survived. When we were small, we were told many stories about the war, and I was very surprised by the fact that they had been able to get by in such difficult times. I know from experience that faith and mutual help can make people strong: I learned that from them. All in all, I can say that the course of my faith was normal, thanks to my family, contacts with priests in the parish, and the missionaries at school.

What was your religious education like?

I breathed the faith first of all in the family. I had a normal family consisting of people who worked hard and brought me up with simple values: faith, family, love for the church, good manners, sound principles. My parents were very active in the church. From my mother I learned to pray, reciting the simple traditional Christian prayers: the Our Father, Hail Mary, the rosary. . . . By the time I was three I knew the main prayers and was able to say the rosary on my own.

There was a tradition in our neighborhood: the statue of Our Lady of Fatima was carried from house to house. It stayed in one house for a week, and that family had to say the rosary. At the end of the week the statue went to another family. I remember the families always invited me to lead the prayers, even though I was very young. I enjoyed it because in that way I went from my house into other people's homes. And after the rosary the families gave me a snack, a piece of cake or a sweet, and of course I enjoyed that a lot.

As I grew up, gradually my family showed me how to become an active member of the Christian community. Our involvement with the life of the community consisted mainly in attending the Sunday Mass and festivals in which we regularly took part. My dad was a member of the Knights of Columbus, while my mother belonged to the Catholic Women's League.[1] Both these organizations promoted charitable initiatives for the poor.

In your childhood and adolescence was there any religious figure you were particularly struck by?

In our parish "Nuestra Señora del Pilar" at Imus, when I was a boy—about thirteen or fourteen—there was a young priest named Father Redentor Corpuz. Our house was a short way away from the cathedral and the town square. So we were on the scene and took part in the great religious, social, and cultural events in Imus. Father Corpuz organized meetings and youth training. In particular I remember that the Columbian Squires, a youth group attached to the Knights of Columbus, were very active. I did not want to join, but my Dad forced me to. In the end I have to say that I'm glad he did, because in that group I became closer and closer to the priests and made many friends. We were involved in many projects: catechism for children, help for the poor communities at Christmas (bringing food, organizing sporting events for kids, and so on). We formed a choir to liven up the Masses (actually, I have quite a good ear for music).

---

1. The Catholic Women's League Philippines, founded in 1957, is an association of lay women that promotes the faith and apostolate within families.

During those years I and others were trained to be leaders under the supervision of Father Corpuz. I was very impressed by his personality. He quite often came to our house, talked to me, and became a good friend. At that age I wondered why that man, who was older than me, wanted to become my friend: what did he find interesting about a boy like me? In fact he introduced me to many of his friends, community leaders. Many were high-level people, and they were all against the dictatorship of President Marcos. I was the youngest of the little group, and I listened attentively to all their discussions about justice, human rights, freedom. . . . I didn't understand it all, but I was interested in these big questions. Those friends of Father Corpuz were very important. In particular, I remember a lady called Yolanda Narvaez, who is now a member of a religious community, Sisters of Social Service.[2] At that time she belonged to a group called Binhi ("Seed"). Some members of that group are still active in the Focolare Movement, for example, Pilar Capistrano, the Erasmo married couple, or they are involved as lay preachers (Mie Joson and Robert Castañeda) or in social work (as in the case of Lina Jacinto).

You yourself have told us that you have experienced popular Fili-pino religiosity since you were a child. If there's one thing that strikes the Western visitor to the Philippines, it is that very wide-

---

2. The Sisters of Social Service are a women's apostolic soci-ety of pontifical right founded in Hungary in 1908.

spread popular religiosity. The people continually go in and out of church; they stand in front of statues of the Madonna, Jesus, or the saints and pray, sometimes out loud with many joining in. How important for you is popular piety?

Some aspects of Filipino popular piety are a legacy from the Spanish presence in our land (the Filipino ecclesiastical jurisdiction began when it was governed by Mexico, [at that time the Vice-Royalty of New Spain]). This remains an aspect of Filipino culture, enjoying physical contact, touch, sight, rituals, music, and people gathering together. The presence of holy pictures and statues maintains this contact and reassures the faithful that God, the Madonna, and the saints are near. The act of touching a holy statue is not idolatry, as outsiders sometimes accuse us, but is an imaginative contact. That is to say: the people know perfectly well that a plaster or wooden statue is not the Lord, just a representation of him. We could say, broadly speaking, that pictures and statues are vicarious or sacramental instruments. Another element to stress is the fact that besides the "official" liturgy, which remains indispensable (Mass, sacraments, etc.), popular devotion is an expression of the initiative and creativity of the poor and simple, as it is more natural and closer to their culture. We should not forget that many forms of popular piety began from below. It was only later that they were recognized by the official authorities of the church.

What does that mean?

It means that popular piety is a vast area for the active participation of poor and simple people, which goes beyond the structure of official groups and committees. In my opinion people's greatest participation in the life of faith takes part through popular piety. And we also see popular piety joining rich and poor together: they are all Filipinos and popular devotion unites them all, beyond social classes and cultural differences. In various ways popular religiosity becomes the symbolic place where faith and culture meet.

How can the church nurture this kind of religious expression?

As pastors we are well aware of the risks that popular piety can have for faith, risks ranging from sentimentalism to syncretism. So we must provide the faithful with a solid biblical, catechetical, and liturgical grounding. Most Filipino Catholics are open to this. Besides, the fervor shown in these devotions is channeled into ordinary parish life, which encourages participation in the various church services.

To give an example: at the celebration of the Black Nazarene of Quiapo,[3] the faithful who come together in the basilica are mainly from the poor areas, and they

---

3. A much-venerated statue representing a dark-skinned Jesus carrying his cross toward Calvary. The image was made by a Mexican artist in the seventeenth century and stands in the minor basilica of the Black Nazarene in Quiapo, a district of Manila.

find a fellow sufferer in the suffering Jesus. They want to touch the statue or even just clutch the rope that is tied to the statue. These are people who have nothing else to hold onto but Jesus. Thanks to the initiative of the parish priest and the local committee organizing the celebration, many of these devout, sick, and suffering people now help others who are poor and sick. In this way, popular piety moves on from being a private individual phenomenon to become service and community action. I must also stress that I myself have been greatly helped by popular religiosity.

When?

During my period of study in the United States from 1987 to 1991, I always prayed the novena to the Madonna of Perpetual Help, to the guardian angels. and to St. Anthony of Padua, a saint who is also very famous in the Philippines. In my own country I was a leader when these celebrations took place, but in the United States I became simply one of the faithful. Nevertheless, I felt a strong cultural and spiritual bond with my people. In the confusion and sadness that sometimes arises when one is alone in a foreign land, faith expressed in terms of popular religiosity is comforting. Now I understand better the people who go every Wednesday to pray to the Madonna of Perpetual Help! While I was living in the United States I also came into contact with the problems suffered by migrants, the difficulty of supporting themselves economically and their families at home. I saw families who were very well off in the Philippines become indigent in the United States. For them and for me, the faith that the risen Lord really makes the sun rise every day became vital—every day. Without faith there was no hope!

2

One Less Doctor, One More Priest

Did you know that the future Cardinal Tagle was only admitted to the seminary "with reservations," that is, with a probation period of six months? This is one of the surprises revealed in his account of his vocation to the priesthood. This is a true story of someone who from boyhood had dreamed of becoming a doctor.

A decisive example in the course of the young Luis Antonio Tagle's vocation was the "priest serving on the margins," Father Redentor Corpuz, a priest who looked after the poor and most deprived, whom Pope Francis would have liked very much. The young man was fascinated by this priest's generous service.

This apparently minor biographical detail also tells a lot about how Cardinal Tagle understands his ministry today: not as the exercise of power or privilege but as dedication to service. "In some cultures," he says, "becoming a seminarian means rising above the rest of humanity. And becoming a deacon means rising even higher. Becoming a priest? Wow! Then you begin to belong to heaven, rather than to Earth. You are seen as someone who goes about with the angels rather than with normal human beings."

But it was not like that for him. His ordination as a priest was not the fulfillment of a long-dreamt-of career. Rather, it was the culmination of a journey that had been anything but straight—a journey undertaken in total obedience to the will of God, who led him to embrace the priesthood even though, as he said, when he was young Luis Antonio Gokim Tagle imagined himself in very different shoes.

But, as we know, God's ways are not always what human beings foresee. In the case of Cardinal Tagle, he himself says that trusting in God led him to total human and spiritual fulfillment.

When you were a boy what did you dream of becoming when you were grown up?

During my adolescence my idea was to become a doctor, and my parents approved of that choice. I believed in it deeply and was interested in medicine (I still am today). At about the age of fourteen I began looking into some medical books. I wanted to prepare straight away for the university admission exam. I had no doubts. "I'll be a doctor," I said to myself. The Scheut Belgian missionaries, with whom I went to school and who ran their own seminary, often gave me books to read about the religious life; they wanted to draw me in that direction. But Father Corpuz, my parish priest, my trusted friend, once said to me: "You're young to be thinking about the priesthood. Better for you to continue with the plan you have in mind; when you're older, then you can decide." I told him firmly: "In any case I'm not interested in the priesthood." And he answered: "Whatever happens, speak to me first about any decision you take." After a little while Father Corpuz was moved to another parish in the diocese, a very poor parish in one of the most devastated areas of Imus. When I went to visit him, I felt sad for him because I saw he was deeply involved in a wretched situation. But that meeting gave rise to a question in me: "Why is that young priest 'wasting' his life in a place like that? A place where, in human terms, it's not worth living?" Father Corpuz's new situation remained a mystery to me.

How did you pursue your plan?

A few years later another priest came and took Father Corpuz's place in our parish. We did not develop the same understanding as there had been between me and his predecessor. But I was the leader of the local Catholic youth organization so I had to have dealings with him and obey him. In 1972 I was fifteen; it was my last year of high school and I was about to choose a university. When the priest heard about my plan (to study medicine) he said to me: "Do you want to become a doctor?" There is a schol-

arship offered by the Jesuits at the Manila Athenaeum.[1]
If your marks are high enough you can try the selection
exam, and if you get through, you will get the scholarship and so you won't pay anything for attending the university." Indeed, my parents could not have afforded the
university fees.

The exam is very competitive: three intensive days of
interviews and tests. That priest entered four boys from
our parish for the exam. I remember that during the first
test there was a question: "Type of Vocation." I did not
understand what it meant, so I went up to the priest
supervising the exam to ask him to explain. And he gave
me an answer that stunned me: it was a normal question,
seeing that this was an exam to enter the seminary. I was
furious. I felt betrayed by my priest, who had tricked me
and pulled a fast one on me. But I was unable to leave that
place during the whole three days. After the exam I went
straight to our parish priest and asked him: "Why did
you do that to me and not tell me the truth?" He replied:
"Given that your mind is focused on medicine, you
haven't taken anything else into consideration, whereas I
want you to look at the whole range of possibilities before
you. Are you sure you want to become a doctor?" I was
absolutely furious with him.

---

1. The Manila Athenaeum University is a famous private
university in the Philippines, from which the ex-presidents
Corazón Aquino and Benigno Aquino III graduated.

But he was absolutely right!

But I have to admit that he had seen clearly. Because after that moment of fury, I fell into a state of confusion. I began to ask myself: "Who do I want to be? What do I really want?" At that moment I began to remember the life led by Father Corpuz: his life of sacrifice, his choice to devote himself to the poor, the new parish where he lived. . . . But I tried to rid my mind of all that: "I'll enroll for medicine! I don't want temptations; medicine is the way for me," I kept telling myself. In fact, sometimes I began to get worried, because out loud I was saying "medicine" but deep in my heart I was hoping to pass the exam for admission to the seminary. But that didn't happen. The priest in charge turned down my request because I was too young.

What was your reaction?

I felt sad and paradoxically the thing disturbed me. In fact, if I really wanted to become a doctor I should not have been upset: that "no" confirmed me in my initial plan. The exam supervisor told me: "We can't admit you to the seminary, but you can study medicine in our pre-university (today the Manila Jesuits have a Faculty of Medicine but at that time they did not). At that time the seminarians also attended various courses in universities which were open to all. I was even more confused; I really didn't know what to do. My parents said: "You can study in the Jesuits' pre-university and then continue with your studies in the state university." But they didn't know that

I had sat for the exam to enter the seminary. I had told them nothing about the "clerical trick" the parish priest had played on me and my furious reaction to it. I was very confused, but they didn't know why. Every day I went to church at 4:30 in the morning to pray to the Lord exposed in the Blessed Sacrament: "Help me!" I begged him. I didn't know what to do.

What happened then?

I consulted a priest in the minor seminary in the diocese of Imus, and he took me to the rector, to whom I explained how things were. "You haven't got a vocation to the priesthood; go to university," was his reply. I went back at least four times to talk to the rector, asking him for a chance to enter the seminary. In vain. The day came that was fixed by the university as the last day for enrollment. I decided to go there and I said to myself: "That's enough thinking about the seminary." I'll go to university, and I'll pay the fees myself." I was in a queue for the faculty counter, when the famous priest whom I had seen during the three days of tests, who had supervised the exam (the one I had asked: "What does 'Type of Vocation' mean?") passed by me and saw me. Recognizing me, he scolded me, why had I insisted on going to the rector to plead my cause? "We sent you a letter to tell you that's enough; don't go anymore." "Yes you did," I confirmed. He said: "What are you going to study?" I answered: "Biology or any other science course. . . ." And he said: "Follow me."

He took me into his office and said to me: "Do you pray?" Have you any friends among the Cavite priests?" I told him about Father Corpuz: I didn't know he had been a classmate of his! To my great surprise, his final decision was: "We will accept you into the seminary but "under supervision" for six months. Come back tomorrow with all your luggage." I was astonished and answered: "But my family doesn't even know about it. . . ." "So phone them!" was his sharp reply.

How did your family receive that decision?

My parents were very surprised by the whole story and also somewhat aggrieved because I had not involved them in my worries. They went on imagining me as a doctor. But they did not put a spoke in my wheels. Next day they came with me to the seminary. The smiling rector welcomed me with these words: "The first lesson you must learn from this whole story is as follows: if you want to get something you have to work hard and sacrifice yourself." That was how my training began, in St. José's seminary, which was situated behind the campus of the Jesuit University in Quezon City (a district of Manila). It was 1973.

Just a year after Marcos had begun the dictatorship stage of his presidency?

I remember the day that Marcos decreed martial law. It was September 21, 1972. All radio and television programs were blocked. The only thing on air was the announcement of the introduction of martial law. It was forbidden to gather in large groups. Criticisms of the government were regarded as subversive and could lead to arrest. The main opposition leaders were thrown into jail, including Senator Benigno Aquino.[2] The rule of law was suspended. We felt like prisoners. At first many people agreed that the country needed martial law to re-establish discipline and internal order. But as time passed, we realized that it all led to abuse of power, suppression of liberty, corruption, and blaming the poor. The seminary taught children their rights, interceded for prisoners, negotiated with the military and police force, and helped the families of the disappeared. That was the atmosphere I found in the seminary.

Let's go back to your studies. You were "on approval" for six months in the seminary. How did you come to continue your studies?

After the first semester I went to the rector and asked him: "Can I come back for the second semester?" He said: "Why are you asking me?" "It was you who told me so when you said that I would be 'under supervision' for six months," I replied. His reply: "Water under the bridge,

---

2. Husband of Corazón Aquino (president of the Philippines from 1986 to 1992) and father of Benigno "Noynoy" Aquino III (president from 2010 until 2016).

just come back." So I attended the four years of philosophy, after which I went on to theology (five years). After the second year of theology, I did a year of pastoral work in various places. One place was an area inhabited by poor people and squatters near Quezon City, and then I went to Cebu, where I did the Spiritual Exercises of St. Ignatius Loyola, which lasted for a month. I was ordained deacon on July 18, 1981. Finally, on February 27, 1982, I was ordained as a priest in the diocese of Imus.

What do you remember about your years in the seminary?

During my time in the seminary I was able to study with great teachers, from whom I learned a lot. One teacher who was important for me was Father Roque Ferriols, a great philosopher. He had translated some books by Gabriel Marcel and other European philosophers into the Filipino language. He was a pioneer in the teaching of Western philosophy in the local language. His slogan was "Give God the best": he did not accept minimalism of any kind.

I can't forget Father Catalino Arevalo, who was regarded as the doyen of Asian philosophy, a Jesuit, the first Asian to be appointed to the International Theological Commission (I was the second Filipino). Arevalo brought liberation theology to the Philippines. It could be said that he was the architect of the theology of FABC (the Federation of Asian Bishops' Conferences). The cornerstones of his thinking were these three important themes:

dialogue with other religions, with other cultures, and with the poor.

Father Eduardo Hontiveros, a Filipino Jesuit, was regarded as the father of Filipino liturgical music. He composed some musical pieces in the local language; he was a close friend and showed me his songs as soon they were "churned out." In February 2014, in the Milan cathedral, when I was presiding over a great Eucharistic celebration with the local Filipino community, I had the treat of hearing that music again which I had heard for the first time in the seminary. It was very emotional! Father Eduardo also taught me to lead the choir, seeing that I had a gift for music (in fact I love to listen to it; I can read music but can't play any instrument).

I remember our spiritual directors, the Jesuits Hernando Maceda and Thomas Green, who taught us the way of prayer and discernment. My rectors, Father Juan Sanz and Father Vicente San Juan, guided me with a gentle but firm hand. Fratel Lorenzo de Vela gave me great help and encouragement. The lay staff at the seminary also became good friends. I am still in contact with some of them. Naturally, my memories of the seminary would not be complete without mentioning my companions. Lastly, the people we met in the various parishes where we served helped us become good priests.

Did you never have doubts about your choice to become a priest?

No, I never doubted my choice, but that wasn't because of the qualities and talents I had to offer as a priest. I am the first to admit my errors and defects. I have no doubts about my decision to become a priest because the strange and convoluted story of how I came to be one helped me understand that my vocation was real: my life did not belong to me! I am here, in this state of life, not through my own choice but by and thanks to the hand of God. I never want to doubt this, even when I run into some difficulty. I can give a little example. While I was writing my doctoral thesis in the United States, the computer crashed and I lost seventy-five pages of my writing. My first thought was: "The Lord doesn't want me to go on studying." Then I telephoned Father Komonchak, my supervisor, to tell him. He said: "Father Tagle, you've already given me a copy of those pages!"

Is the priesthood still an attractive ideal for young Filipinos?

In general the priesthood remains an attractive ideal in the Philippines, but often it is too "idealized." Young men feel afraid of the demands of priestly life and say: "I'm not worthy or capable of reaching that ideal." Priesthood must remain an ideal of spirituality and service, because otherwise there is the danger of succumbing to the temptation to choose it in order to gain a higher standard of living than normal, with social, cultural and religious benefits. That's a real danger. So the question is: how to keep the ideal of priesthood alive without falling into the temptation of a false idea of the priestly life.

So what do you do to get "pastors smelling of the sheep"?

We need priests and religious who are faithful to their spirituality and to the pastoral dimension of priesthood, and who have a truly "human" face. That balance between a very high ideal, but embodied in flesh and blood, makes the priesthood attractive. So seminaries, training courses, and summer camps are not enough to promote vocations—of course, they all help—but it is also necessary for young people to see that ideal embodied and lived up to by priests who are very human and active.

If we move from the Philippines to the West, we can't fail to see that vocations to the priesthood are drastically decreasing. What do you think about this?

This is a phenomenon we are beginning to understand because, according to the experts, the fall in vocations in the West is linked to various "isms": consumerism, materialism, secularism. . . . I believe these cultural phenomena have a profound effect on the values of families and the young. Young people are very vulnerable. Psychologists tell us that adolescents want above all to be accepted and welcomed. And the way they are accepted has an effect on their choice of life. At the same time, the witness—for example of their family, priests they know—is also important. For of course, not all young people's "inner" spaces are filled with other cultural forces driving them to make different choices. Family and church have a space in young people's hearts and minds, but the question to ask ourselves is: do family and church "fill" that space or do they leave it empty for other forces to enter?

Besides, I believe we are also feeling the renewing breath of the Holy Spirit. In the history of the church, renewal comes together with death: think of the paschal mystery. We must look at things in a wider perspective: in other parts of the world, especially in the new churches, we are experiencing an exceptional flowering of vocations.

3

Priests to Learn from the Poor

When Luis Antonio Gokim Tagle became a priest, the Philippines, under the dictatorship of Marcos, was going through a dramatic period: social tension was very high. But the young priest—supported by the example of his bishop, Felix Perez, an outstanding figure in the Filipino church—did not give way to circumstances and threw himself headlong into pastoral work. Urged on by Perez, he explored new ways to preach the gospel and do pastoral work: "Let's Try" was the motto of that period, expressing the will to move off the habitual beaten track to seek innovative and more effective methods to reach people's hearts.

The bishop had realized straight away that Tagle had uncommon gifts for spiritual leadership and entrusted him with delicate educational tasks in the seminary: first as spiritual father, then as rector, despite his young age (twenty-five). Tagle himself tried to get out of these jobs, citing his lack of experience. But Monsignor Perez proved to be farsighted and encouraged him to accept.

In the seminary Father Tagle, backed by the bishop, introduced a series of significant changes: he set up mini base com-

munities and introduced a style of simplicity, with relaxed, not too formal relations between seminarians and teachers, who shared small everyday tasks such as washing the dishes.

In 1982, Tagle began his academic teaching career. He was called to teach theology in Manila at the tender age of twenty-five. Tagle brought youthful and characteristic enthusiasm to the task and was not daunted by the intense rhythm his days acquired (he got up at 4 a.m. and travelled to Manila by bus, twenty-five kilometers in the chaotic traffic of the Asian capital). During the course of his life this academic experience was to become more and more important.

Your route through the seminary ended with your ordination. . . .

But first I'd like to talk about my ordination as a deacon: it was on July 18, 1981. On that day there was almost a typhoon, a very strong wind. We had no electricity in the church and were almost in the dark. The one other candidate and I met in St. José's seminary in Manila, with our respective families and friends. My fellow candidate was from the diocese of Manila (now I am its archbishop). It was Felix Perez, the bishop of Imus, who ordained us. In such difficult weather conditions my first thought was about that wind, whether it was the presence of the Holy Spirit or the resistance of the devil wanting to prevent my ordination. Because of the bad weather the whole celebration ran late; the bishop himself arrived late. When at last he arrived, he told me: "I've forgotten everything necessary for the celebration: my miter, my crosier, my Pontifical [Bishops' Liturgy Book[3]]. . . ." And I said to myself: my clerical life is beginning with this absentmindedness. . . . But it was a very simple ceremony with a bit of a tempest!

On February 27, 1982 you became a priest. What was that day like?

I was happy but also rather stunned, confused, and I felt humble. From the group of seminarians who had begun philosophy together, I was the only one who had reached ordination. And that's a mystery: I was the last to be accepted, as I explained before, but the only one to stay till the end, till ordination. I felt all this was truly like a mystery, but I did not understand its meaning. On my ordination day I joked with the Jesuit father, the one in charge of exams in the seminary and who had originally said I was too young. I said to him: "If you hadn't accepted me, this year we would have zero ordinations." I experienced that day as one of serene joy, but at the same time I did not understand everything that was happening to me. There was a good turn-out of so many priests, not only from Imus: my teachers and various religious. My grandparents were there, including my Chinese grand-

---

3. The *Pontificale Romanum* (Roman Pontifical) is the Catholic Latin liturgical book that contains the rites performed by bishops.

father, who was still alive. I was the twenty-seventh priest ordained since the foundation of the diocese.

What, in particular, do you remember most about your ordination?

There was a small "incident" during the Mass. We had organized the liturgy at least a month beforehand with the master of ceremonies. We had chosen Psalm 8 for the responsorial psalm, which praises the Lord for the beauty of creation. The refrain had been written by Father Corpuz, my parish priest when I was a boy. But the music had been composed by Father Eduardo Hontiveros, the initiator of Filipino liturgical music. That was the program planned. But when the soloist, a seminarian, began singing the psalm, it wasn't the one we had planned! I didn't understand; I didn't recognize the music. But after I had read the third line of words, I was surprised. "Who has found this prayer?" I asked myself. It was a prayer written by me during the month of Spiritual Exercises.

In 1979 my fellow seminarians and I had made a thirty-day spiritual retreat, during which a grave crisis occurred: in the first week one of us had suffered a nervous collapse. So, to encourage my comrades, I had shared with them a reflection on the prophet Hosea: "When Israel was a child, I loved her. How could I forsake you, Ephraim?" One night I copied out that prayer and gave it to my comrades. But I had completely forgotten about it. But one of my comrades kept the prayer, gave it to Father Hontiveros, who set it to music and that was what was sung during my ordination. That prayer reminded me of so many things: the crisis in the seminary, what happened to our comrade, who later committed suicide; suffering, the Lord's love. . . .

Who were the church personalities who influenced you most as a young priest?

First and foremost the person who influenced me was Monsignor Felix Perez, bishop of Imus, the one who ordained me as deacon and priest. A simple and humble pastor, he was the one who implemented Vatican II in the diocese. He ensured its openness to the novelties introduced by the Council and the renewal of the diocesan church structure to bring it in line with the spirit of Vatican II, with particular attention to the renewal of the clergy.

But he was also a prophetic voice against the dictatorship and for peace. He was a member of a group of seven bishops who had strongly criticized Marcos's regime. This included, among others, the Jesuit bishop Francisco Claver, the Carmelite Julio Labayan, and Archbishop Carmelo Morelos.

Perez had a great influence on young priests. In my case his presence and his teaching had been with me since I was a seminarian. Perez was a free spirit. And because of his inner freedom, he was a creative person in his pastoral choices. It was he who taught me pastoral creativity. For example, he tried to write catechisms for children, for married couples, for fishermen. He often repeated: "Let's try." He loved trying out new ways to proclaim the gospel so that it reached everyone. He was a very brave person in defense of the poor.

I remember how Bishop Perez led the poor who had lost their homes and marched toward the government office responsible for housing. One day the police stopped a march led by Monsignor Perez. Some officers grasped their weapons. Various priests joined in with the bishop and the crowd. With my own ears I heard Bishop Perez saying, "Before firing on the people you should fire on the bishop."

Bishop Perez also encouraged me to study seriously and to deepen my knowledge of Filipino culture in order to find a way to link it with the contents of the Christian faith. He often said to me, "How would you explain Christian doctrine to these people?" He challenged me to apply the faith to the various situations that a priest may find himself in.

"Applying the faith to various situations." Is that something you still try to do today?

Of course. Today as a bishop I am always asking myself how to present the faith in a way that is relevant and true to life. The great lesson of my pastoral life has been to go to the poor, not bringing my own words, but having a heart ready to listen and learn from them. Before saying a word, it is important to understand the person before you, understand him or her by listening respectfully in a way that also respects their dignity. Only after that do I feel I have the right to say anything. Of course, I have the word of God in mind, the Bible, the social teaching of the church, which I can share with them. But for me the best way to draw the poorest people is this: to raise their dignity by listening to them.

What does that mean in practice?

I find I often have to change what I plan to say, my analysis of the situation, my prepared text, on the basis of what I am confronted with. When I was younger I went to meetings overprepared, with my prepackaged analysis, my questions and answers. But over the years I have discovered that my questions do not always coincide with those the people are asking. Their needs are not what I had imagined they would be. First of all I have to listen. For me this is a challenge, not only for pastors but also for all those who are engaged in preaching the gospel. Not to come with easy answers but to bring an attitude of solidarity and humble listening.

What post were you given after your ordination?

Shortly after my first Mass, Monsignor Perez said to me one day: "Within three years I am sending you abroad to gain a doctorate in theology." I thought to myself, "I bet he forgets." Then for my first post he appointed me vicar of the parish of San Agostino in the municipality of Mendez. The people there were mainly employed in agriculture (especially growing coffee); the population consisted of very simple people, great workers and with strong faith. I officially entered the parish on Palm Sunday 1982.

After only three weeks Bishop Perez phoned me urgently: he was ill and wanted me to take his place in giving the Spiritual Exercises to the seminarians who were preparing for ordination as priests. I replied, "But I am young, barely twenty-five." He answered, "Go all the same. Speak about your experience during your month of retreat as a seminarian." The bishop had only conducted the meditations for the first week, and I had to preach for the next three weeks!

Immediately after the retreat he appointed me spiritual director of the seminary, and I kept my parish job as well. During that same period the Divine Word missionaries (Verbites) also asked me to teach philosophy and theology in their school. I accepted and told myself I would be a teacher in my free time. I got stuck in these three jobs, each of which was so different: pastoral work in direct contact with the people, training seminarians, and academic work and teaching.

Is there any particular episode you remember from your experience as a parish priest in Imus?

The first episode that comes to mind relates to the parish school. It was in 1998. I had been appointed parish

priest of the Imus cathedral in 1998. During the following year, in preparation for the 2000 Grand Jubilee, I set
up a retreat for the leaders and co-ordinators of the base
communities in the parish, a fine group of people. At the
end of the retreat (it was during the Christmas period) I
asked them a question: What kind of manger would the
Lord want to find in our parish life if he was born today in
Imus? For me this was only a question for reflection, but
the group took it very seriously. Next day they came to
present me with an actual plan for our parish. That community had quite a few newcomers who came in search
of work from other areas of the Philippines. They had
made their decision and said to me, "We haven't got a
Catholic school in our parish for the Christian and human
education of our children." I replied, "Λ school? No! We
haven't got the land, the space; it costs a lot; we haven't
got the resources! It's not something we can do, even
though it's a good idea!" For a whole year that group of
leaders came every week to tell me we needed to make
that plan happen and I always answered, "No, no, no!"
In the end to bring the matter to a conclusion, I took them
to Bishop Sobreviñas. I wanted the bishop to put a defi-
nite end to the project. After half an hour the bishop came
out with these words: "OK, Father Tagle, begin the school
in June." It was spring. I said, "But your Excellency, our
agreement was to say no." We two had spoken together
beforehand, but he had forgotten our plan. It was mad-
ness. It was Easter and he wanted the school to be opened
in June. That day I could not deny the persistence of the

laity, over a whole year. Neither could I deny that inspiration had come in a spiritual moment. This was not just a decision taken in theory; we were really dealing with the action of the Holy Spirit.

In short, you had to give in.

I told that group: "All right, we'll begin the school in June. I agree to take part in this plan but on certain conditions: first, the school will be mainly for poor children, so that their families have the chance of a high quality education in a human and Christian atmosphere. Second, so many of you are teachers. I want you to become voluntary teachers! The families who come will have to fill in a form marking one of five options for how much they can pay." So between 1998 and 2000 we began the school in a room in the parish pastoral center with twenty children from the nursery school. When we had no money, the teacher phoned me and said, "Father, we need money." And I replied, "Let's pray together to the Madonna, St. Joseph, and St. Anthony of Padua." And straight away the money came in. In the second year more children came. We took over a garage belonging to the administration to use as another classroom. News of the school spread, and a rich family in the parish phoned me. "Father, is it true that you have started a school for the poor?" "Yes, it's true." "We want to make a donation of land." When, months later, I presented the plan to the Presbyteral Council, the diocesan officer for schools replied to me, "Father Tagle, you have just presented the formula for the failure of any school. The school must be business-like." Well, today that school is still the largest parochial school in the diocese of Imus, with more than two thousand students. And everything happened through donations, charity, and solidarity.

From being spiritual director of the seminary you then became rector.

A year after I became a priest (we are going back to 1982) the rector of the Imus seminary suddenly had a heart attack. I remember well. It was the first anniversary of my ordination, and I was with my parents for a little party. The bishop phoned me unexpectedly, telling me that I was immediately to take the place of the sick priest and appointed me, on the spot, as *ad interim* rector. I tried to resist, pointing out my young age and inexperience. I was only twenty-six years old and I have only been ordained as a priest for a year! But the bishop tried to calm me down: "It's only a short-term job." And that's how it was in May of that year. Meanwhile I continued serving my parish. In June when the new academic year was about to begin, the bishop phoned me again, to ask me to continue in the post of *ad interim* rector, because the rector had to go to the United States for a surgical operation. Although very much aware of my limitations, I accepted.

As an educator in the seminary I was completely alone. I learned to listen to the seminarians, to be with them, becoming friends with them, but able—when necessary—to be firm. Once I had grasped the bishop's vision for the church—he wanted to bring the teachings and decisions of the Second Vatican Council into our diocese—I tried my best to put them into practice among the seminarians, who were future priests. I realized that the church renewal proposed by Vatican II had to be tried out from the seminary onward. Vatican II should not only be studied but put into practice in pastoral programs, and in the seminary's own structures and community. I wanted the young seminarians to make it their own before they became priests and started work in parishes.

Then you became rector definitively. You could bet on it.

From June 1983 until May of the following year I continued to be *ad interim* rector. In June 1984 the rector decided not to return for health reasons, and the bishop appointed me rector of the seminary effective immediately. I was only twenty-seven, and in the group of seminarians to be ordained priests that year all (except one) were older than I! I tried to object to Bishop Perez: "I don't see myself as rector." The bishop replied, "I have consulted the seminarians and they agree." And he added, smiling, "You will make fewer mistakes than others." He didn't say, "You will do better than others."

What do you remember in particular from that period?

That year I learned from the bishop to plan certain education options together. It was a great experience, because we were trying out new things together. It was he who said, "Let's try . . ." For example, we tried to set up small base communities in the seminary. How? Eight seminarians lived in each corridor. We invited them to pray together, to share their money a bit, and to live in common. Then they did preaching work together among the poor, helping out in some workers' communities. During that period we introduced work sharing among the seminarians and the paid staff: of the cooking, laundry, caretaking, etc. We said to ourselves, why should these people eat at a distant table and not sit down with us, priests and seminarians? Every Friday there was a meeting of the base community of workers living in the seminary. The seminarians were asked to reflect with them. It was a practical way to promote the dignity of the poor. So we thought of the seminary as a family. We priests ate together with the seminarians, not in a separate place. All of us in turn, including the priests, cleaned the common rooms and washed the dishes. For the seminarians this sort of thing was a conversion experience, for in that way they learned to live among ordinary people.

During the years that you were an educator the Philippines was under the military dictatorship. What did it mean to educate young people, future priests, living under a military regime?

In order to stem the violent opposition to Marcos, we supported a nonviolent movement in the parishes, and we gave its members a Christian education on the values of

justice, freedom and peace. Freedom and human and civil
rights were suspended by the dictatorship. For example,
meetings of more than three or four people were forbidden. The Filipino church always had a clear program line,
defined as "critical collaboration." Part of the church,
including some bishops, found the situation too confusing
and thought that the country needed a strong leader. This
group of bishops, however, hoped that the dictatorship
would be short term. But there was also another group of
people in the church who were more critical than collab-
orative, because they saw the risks of power and money.
That is, there was a small group in the church, which
included priests and religious, who sympathized with
the extreme left with a hard-line ideology. For example,
in the seminary this ideological division existed between
the teachers and also the students. As rector of the seminary I followed the directive of Bishop Perez: pastoral
spirituality includes the defense of human rights, but it is
spirituality not ideology.

How did you try to keep to this via media *in practice?*

In my position in the parish and in the seminary I tried
to organize the poor, especially the peasants, to rescue
them from their vulnerability to armed groups such as
the New People's Army (NPA).[4] It was easy for this group

---

4. Armed wing of the Filipino Communist Party with a Mao-
ist orientation.

to draw the peasants into their ideology and violence. For example, in my first parish we organized an agricultural co-operative so that farmers could sell their products directly to the market, which meant they got more for them and were more independent. We also took a lot of care of the young. We were very aware of the protests, for indeed, they wanted to organize public demonstrations in the square. We gave them these instructions: "It is prohibited to use any propaganda language, flags, or political or ideological slogans. But it is not prohibited to use organized liturgical singing." So we organized a singing competition, a contest, with the *sotto voce* condition: the content of the songs must have a social meaning. We took part in so many demonstrations, but always in an original and nonviolent way. For example, in a large demonstration in the square (in 1984), instead of placards and ideological slogans, we raised rosaries. The idea for this gesture came from a group led by us priests. This group worked for social reforms in a nonviolent way, following the inspiration of the gospel. We were still far from the 1986 "rosary revolution," when two million people marched through the main streets of Manila, but what went before that was a sort of preparation.

How did you live as a young priest?

I forced myself to live in a simple way. I did not have my own office; I met people from time to time wherever there was space. I did not want to become a prisoner in one room! I didn't have a car, I always travelled by bus. I went by public transport from Tagaytay to Manila—an eighty-kilometer journey—to teach theology. For from 1982 the archbishop of Manila, Cardinal Jaime Sin, and the rector of the St. Carlo Major Seminary, the auxiliary bishop Gaudencio Rosales (who later became a cardinal), had asked my bishop to allow me to teach theology one day a week in the Manila seminary. I left at four o'clock in the morning to get to Manila early, thereby avoiding the infernal metropolitan traffic. In the afternoon I went to the Jesuits to teach. They were intense days. I have to say that the word "rest" doesn't exist in my family's dictionary!

Now that you are a bishop, what is your relationship with the seminary and its teachers?

I still continue today to teach in the San Carlo diocesan seminary in Manila and in the Loyola School of Theology, also in Manila, for three hours a week. I teach dogmatic theology: in the first semester I teach the theology of priesthood in the Loyola School, in the second semester I teach dogmatic theology and the theology of priesthood in the San Carlo seminary. Although I have a lot of duties as bishop, I want to keep up this teaching. First, because it "forces" me to read, to go to the library, explore theology. Second, because it is a way of keeping in touch with the generation of future priests. Not all the seminarians I teach come from Manila, because other suffragan dioceses send their students to our diocese. But for me, it's a special moment because I am with them in a different environment from the liturgy or a formal meeting between bishop and seminarians. It's a freer time: yes, I'm still their bishop, but in that situation I am a theology teacher and I open up a space for questions, a personal style that is familiar but also scientific.

However if I compare the time I was able to devote to theology and to the seminarians when I was bishop of Imus with today when I am in Manila, it is very, very different. At that time I lived in the seminary and ran my courses. But this relationship with young students in the seminary remains something very important for me.

In the light of your experience, what do you think are the human and spiritual gifts needed by an educator whose task is to help seminarians along the road to priesthood?

In my experience, first of all, he must be a friend of the seminarians. A friend who knows the way and guides the seminarians with kindness. A friend who listens, who enables them not to hide the truth about their lives. When the seminarians regard a trainer or teacher as a judge, they shut themselves up within. And for me that closing off becomes one of the great dangers preventing us from guiding the young toward full maturity. So an educator must be firm and know how to lead but must also have a lot, a lot of humanity. He must be a friend, father, and brother. The way of discernment, to my way of thinking, is above all co-discernment: the seminarian must know that he is responsible for discerning the will of the Lord. But he must also know that he has a strong help beside him. Moreover, an educator must be a priest who loves his ministry in the seminary. Unfortunately, there are many priests in the seminary who are there only through "obedience," but with heavy hearts. And the seminarians realize they are not there by their own choice.

As a former seminary teacher, what advice would you give to educators today who for a good while now have had to come to grips with the very serious problem of clergy pedophilia?

I was also thinking of these problems when I said just now that the educator must be a friend, encourage co-discernment, and be a cheerful leader. It isn't easy to know seminarians well. Tendencies to commit abuse have mysterious roots, and sometimes even the person himself doesn't know why he is behaving in that way. But when these tendencies break out and come to light, they create fear and shame. In an educational environment that atmosphere of trust and confidence is very important because—in my small experience—when a seminarian has not found a priest or spiritual director to whom he can open up with confidence, he hides things away and does not seek help. Then when he has become a priest, and the tendencies break out, he does not have the strength to confront them. However, today in seminaries we need the help of experts in human sciences, psychologists for example.

4

Theology, a Second Love

Luis Antonio Gokim Tagle has for some time now been one of Asia's cutting-edge theologians. He has not pursued an academic career on his own initiative, however, but agreed to become a theologian at the request of others. He himself made a point of telling us that more than once: he had not expected to devote himself so intensely to theology when he chose the priesthood. Nevertheless . . . seven years of study in the United States, another nine as a teacher in the Philippines in various church and academic centers. All that, together with consultancies, conferences, lectures, have made him a noted figure in church culture worldwide.

*When he was just forty, he was summoned by John Paul II and his theological right-hand man, Joseph Ratzinger, to become part of the International Theological Commission, a think tank that supports the pope on questions of faith and doctrine for the universal church. The following year, in 1998, he was appointed an "expert" (*peritus *in church language) to the Synod of Asia. Then in 2005 he became the youngest bishop (at forty-eight) in the Synod of Bishops devoted to the Eucharist.*

That might have been enough to go to his head. Instead, Professor Tagle kept a very low profile. During his period as a teacher, he published no work of theology, which shows what an "anti-celebrity" he was (and is). His first book, It Is the Lord! *(2003), was printed by the Filipino Jesuits, almost without him knowing. His second,* Easter People*, was published only because some enthusiastic nuns had transcribed his meditations during various spiritual retreats.*

Tagle certainly has a high respect for theology, but he is very far from the image of the scholar shut away in an ivory tower and sick with self-absorption. On one occasion he pointed to the Samaritan woman in John's gospel as a model preacher of the gospel. Professor Tagle pointed out that she had not studied at the Gregorian in Rome: "Jesus taught her by a well for water, not in a school of theology."

For Tagle theology is, of course "talking about God," not in a purely academic way, but as a passionate, continual, daily effort to make God's presence alive and eloquent in the world we live in. In other words, theology as service to the church, not as the practice of an abstruse, self-referential science that fences off knowledge about God and artificially boxes it up in arid definitions, to be distributed to an initiated few. For Tagle, the reader will have already realized that speaking about God means reading salvation history, not only in the scriptures but in the bible of daily life, in workaday meetings, face to face with people, in great and small events in one's own life (and that of others).

What means most to Tagle is to argue—also intellectually—that Christianity "suits" the man and woman of every age. To that effect, Tagle jokingly tells one of his many anecdotes. "One day a social psychology lecturer at the University of Manila told me about the millions of pesos a multinational company in the food sector had paid their department for advice about how to grasp the psychology of the average Filipino. Or, how to reach the minds and hearts of Filipinos, particularly the young, so that they would buy that company's hamburgers. So, before selling their products, that company, like many others, tries to penetrate the world of values, the mentality, tastes, and culture of possible customers."

Well, communicating God is obviously a very different matter from launching a commercial product on the market. But the theologian also has the problem of tuning in to those he is addressing. So the point is that for Tagle, theology has been and is an attempt to enter ever more deeply into the mystery of Christ in order to present him to those who do not know him well enough (or even at all). To enable them to love him.

Why were you sent abroad to study theology?

In 1984, shortly after I had been appointed rector, Bishop Perez phoned me again to tell me that at the end of the academic year I would go abroad to study. "He hasn't forgotten what he said to me," I told myself with regret, as I remembered his promise of a few years before. I replied to him, "There are other priests who are older than I who want to study abroad." "Yes, I know," he answered, "but that's why I'm phoning because you want to come back to your diocese and they don't." "But we've only just begun doing some good things in the seminary." And he said, "Do you believe in the Holy Spirit?" This seminary began without you and will continue without you." End of discussion.

Destination Washington, Catholic University of America. How was that destination chosen?

Monsignor Perez had chosen my possible teachers: the Dominican Christoph Schönborn at Fribourg in Switzerland and the Jesuit Avery Dulles in Washington, DC. (years later both of them were appointed cardinals) and also Joseph Komonchak in Washington. The Jesuit Father Catalino Arevalo, dean of theology in Manila and my ex-teacher, had written to all three of them to introduce me to the theological universities in Fribourg and Washington. The bishop explained to me, "The choice will fall on which one replies first with an offer of a scholarship." So it was Washington that was the quickest. That's how in 1985 I left the Philippines—it was August 11—for the United States. It was a choice that cost me a lot, because I was unsure how long I would be far from my country (two years for the degree and another four for the doctorate). *En passant,* a little while ago I met Cardinal Schönborn in the Vatican and said to him, "If you had replied first, I would have come to Fribourg to study with you." And we had a good laugh!

In the course of my stay in America I had several important teachers, such as Dulles, whom I mentioned before, as well as Father David Power, an Oblate, Professor Francis Schüssler Fiorenza, Sister Elizabeth Johnson, Father Patrick Granfield, Father John Ford, Father John Galvin, Professor Robin Darling, and Father Joseph Komonchak, a specialist in the theology of Bernard Lonergan and theology of the church. He is the editor of the English language edition of the monumental *History of Vatican II* edited by Giuseppe Alberigo. When Professor Alberigo was looking for someone from Asia to contribute an article to his history of the Council, Komonchak gave him my name. My contribution focused on the so-called black week, which was part of my doctoral thesis researching Paul VI and Vatican II. Komonchak became the supervisor of my thesis. Thanks to him I joined the editorial committee for Giuseppe Alberigo's *History of Vatican II.* I wanted to study the Council, and in agreement with Komonchak, we had chosen Paul VI to study. Once, at the beginning of the 1990s, he took me with him to a conference in Lyons, and it was on that occasion that he pointed out my name to Alberigo, who wanted to set up an international committee in Bologna to study the Second Vatican Council. Another of my more noted teachers was Dulles. He taught dogmatics, but about three years after my arrival he retired.

What did you go to study in America?

My study plan was to go deeper into the theology of Vatican II. Monsignor Perez, my bishop in Imus, wanted to set up a theological faculty for this. That is why he sent various local priests abroad to study different theological disciplines (Bible, liturgy, etc.). I got dogmatic theology. In particular, he wanted me to concentrate on ecclesiology, because our basic question at that time was: how can we become a renewed church according to the spirit of the Council? Monsignor Perez did not want random "experiments," but a genuine renewal, founded upon solid theology.

Where did you live in Washington?

I lived in the school house of the Oblate Missionaries of Mary Immaculate, just in front of the university. At that time they had only four Oblate seminarians. The house was half empty, and so it was open to university students. I was the only Filipino guest.

The Filipino embassy was in Washington. And after the end of the dictatorship (1986), the then-ambassador, Emmanuel Pelaez, organized meetings among Filipinos to help the community repair the divisions between Marcos supporters and opponents. The ambassador asked me to help him organize these meetings. I accepted. I saw that on the various occasions at which I was present—such as the blessing of a new residence, a new car, or a religious anniversary—the priest became the visible point of communion among those present. There were all sorts of different people among the Filipinos in Washington: there was a group who had requested political asylum because of the Marcos dictatorship, but also others who were close to the dictator.

I also collaborated with other people who, again with the ambassador's help, had organized a school of Filipino culture for immigrants' children born in the United States, to teach them the language, culture, and music of their home country. I was very busy with this activity on weekends. But my first task remained my studies: every day I studied for at least six hours, as well as attending lectures.

How did you get on in America in such a different environment from home?

There was great freedom for research at the Catholic University of America and plenty of opportunity to formulate your own position. Dialogue and argument were continually promoted. For example, on some occasions when Dulles, a noble and marvelous person, heard a student offering a thought or an argument he considered profound, he said without embarrassment: "By listening to you I have learned something from you."

What else did you see in the United States, besides Washington? Did you visit other states?

During the summer I didn't manage to travel much, because the missionary institutes were looking for priests for their activities and I offered my services to an organization that helped the missionaries. They sent me to Nebraska and Connecticut to speak in the parishes. And then, I didn't have the money to go on holiday! The day I left Imus, my bishop Perez gave me $200; the diocese could not afford more. So, to support myself during my studies, I agreed to type texts for other students in the university. That suited me. I put up a notice on a faculty wall to say that I was available. I got a dollar a page. Then I also worked in the university library, cataloguing books. Incidentally, in the consistory at which I was made a cardinal, in 2012, Chiyono Sata, who had then been in charge of cataloguing the university library, came to Rome because she remembered me, and we greeted each other warmly!

Did you also do pastoral work?

I was involved in pastoral work in the parish of St. Stephen in Washington. The parish priest, who was Irish, was looking for priests to help him celebrate Masses. He particularly welcomed volunteer clerics from poor countries, so that he could support us with money to live on while we were in America. I have to admit that I was rather a favorite of his; he preferred me to the other priests. Every Sunday after the midday Mass, the parish offered anyone who wanted an hour of catechism. I was given the job of running it. The parish priest was also an immigrant who had come from abroad, from Ireland. So it was plain to see that he felt for those who were not American and came from another country. The parish community was extremely kind and welcoming toward people. In the early morning bread and coffee were served to homeless men and women. I liked that very much. Some members of the parish choir were Filipinos, and so the Sunday Mass was an opportunity to meet these compatriots.

What other experiences did you have during your stay in the United States?

I also did voluntary work in a hostel run by the Missionaries of Charity, Mother Teresa of Calcutta's nuns. For a year and a half on two afternoons a week, I went to their reception house. The Catholic University of America is in a poor area, in the northeast section of the city. Walking the streets round the faculty, I saw so many poor people, especially African Americans, as well as many abandoned children and old people. When I began writing my doctoral thesis, I thought it was a good idea to get into contact with these poor people in order to avoid becoming lost in abstractions. That is why I chose to go and do volunteer work with Mother Teresa's nuns, whom I regard as true and genuine witnesses to missionary charity. I went there as a normal volunteer. The superior, an Indian nun, knew I was a priest. At the beginning of the afternoon I went to her and she assigned me my task. One day she said to me: "Today the Lord is calling you to the kitchen to cook the food." I answered her, "But I only know how to make supper for myself." She said: "Well, just cook more of it!" And

I said, "OK. But I only know how to cook Filipino dishes."
"No problem, I'll tell the guests that today we are having
Chinese food!" And indeed the guests ate the lot up!

*During the 1980s AIDS began to claim its first victims. How did
you encounter this disease and those who had it?*

In that experience I touched the sick people's wounds
with my hands, and also those of their families. One of
our jobs as volunteers was to tell the family when a sero-
positive person was going to die. We helped them with
our prayers and then, when the patient died, we took
care of laying out the body. One day we told a family
that their family member was about to die. When they
arrived, they came out of the room almost at once, blurt-
ing out, "But he's not dead yet! Call us when he's dead!"
It was a very sad case. At that time anyone who had con-
tracted AIDS suffered a very strong stigma. For me, sit-
ting by the beds of those sick people, who were often
very lonely, was a religious experience. At least at the
moment of their final meeting with the Lord the Christian community should be beside them. It isn't easy, but
it was something that enriched me both spiritually and
pastorally. I remember when a person with AIDS came
into the room of a sick person who was about to die and
could no longer speak. I was at the bedside of that person who was dying. The AIDS patient said to the dying
man, "When you meet Jesus, tell him we love him. We
love you too. Goodbye, dear friend." That evening those

who were suffering and ill taught me, a doctoral student, simple love and trust.

A cardinal who has done voluntary work in a hostel for the home-less is not something one would normally imagine.

Well, I remember the case of a certain Mr. Brown. He had senile dementia and never wanted to take a shower. The superior asked me to help him have a shower, but he kept escaping. Finally, I managed to corner him and put him under the shower. I turned on the water, but I got completely soaked while he stayed dry! My relationship with the old people there made a deep impression on me because I was thinking that one day my parents would be like them.

How would you sum up your American experience?

The years I spent in the United States were an important experience to get to know another culture, different from my own, from the inside. In Asia we are accustomed to talking about dialogue between cultures. My years in Washington were for me a prolonged experience of being inserted into a different culture. Beginning with the language. I already spoke English, but I had to make a big effort to understand and speak American English, which has particular historical associations that I was unaware of and did not get. Living abroad for some years, in America, gave me new insight into Filipino culture. When we are away from our values and habits we come to understand them better. For example, Asian culture has a lot to do with touching, but the first time I touched an American while we were talking, he withdrew sharply and I was amazed! Or, when I celebrated the anniversary of my ordination as a priest, I invited an American seminarian to lunch in a restaurant. In our Filipino culture, when you invite someone for a meal it's up to you to pay the bill. But that seminarian insisted on paying for his own lunch. These may be small things, but they reveal the wonderfully different ways of seeing the world.

In the United States I learned to be aware of different cultural sensibilities. In short, I understand my own culture better from having been with others belonging to a different cultural tradition. I discovered that what we have in common and the things that are different are a richness for all humanity and also for the church. Life is not monochrome, there is always something different to look at every day.

Besides that, I appreciate my "initiation" into American feminist theology and ecological spirituality. Given the theology department's choice to use inclusive language, I had to watch my English. It was like learning a new language. But all in all it was not just a matter of words, but of broadening my own mind and heart so that more people (women, the poor, the marginalized, the Earth itself) were included in our talk, rather than being excluded.

Washington is also the seat of American political power. Did you have anything to do with that?

Yes, it's true, Washington is a city at the center of politics and power. And during my American years I discovered some alarming aspects of politics, which worried me greatly, especially considering the repercussions they have internationally. I had a number of opportunities to speak to people working in international institutions. From these I got a clear perception that development programs promoted at the world level did not always take care of the poor. On the contrary, it seemed to me that such models always favored those in power, and I didn't like that at all! I recall some military interventions in certain countries and regions of the world, which I thought were not the best solution. Or the calls to some nations to pursue democratic routes that might be practicable in the West, but which in other countries needed to find ways of becoming compatible with the local culture.

On the other hand, I should mention aspects of American culture that I appreciated. I am thinking of the sense of justice that exists in the society and between people and the role of law. There were also some surprising and interesting discoveries for me. For example, in the parish of St. Stephen, the singer who led the singing at Mass was not a Catholic but simply the most qualified person who had sought that type of work. That is a lesson on giving equal opportunities and according to merit.

How did you imagine yourself as a priest? Perhaps going to the West to study was seen as a privilege for a priest from a poor country like the Philippines?

When I decided to enter the seminary, my dream was to become a simple priest in a community of poor people. That vision remains an integral part of the way I see myself today. But I always knew I was available for anything in the church. And in fact the Lord had a different plan for me. But I have not forgotten my vocation to be a servant of the poor. Besides, already in the seminary I had shown I had gifts and talents for study; I was very interested in theology, but my priority remained contact with people. When I was a seminarian one of my teachers often said to me: "I always see you with young people, have you got time to study?" Then after the exams, when we got our marks, I told him, "Father, I did study well, didn't I?" Then, when Bishop Perez told me at the end of the theology course that my professors had recommended me for study, I refused: "That's enough studying, I want to do something else!" But the bishop insisted, and I went to America.

To put the previous question in a different way, isn't it a form of careerism to go and study abroad?

For me leaving my country to study was not a promotion or a career move. No! It was a decision against my will. I only went through obedience and trust in my bishop and professors. Now I understand the experiences of the Old Testament prophets a bit better; they often refused God's call. I never expressed my own will; it was at the request of my superiors that I changed my plans and wishes. But that's all right. And it was like a sort of medicine for me, because it did not make me forget my original vocation to a simple life. For indeed, theologians ought to smell of sheep a bit more. And we hope that the flock might smell a bit more of Christ thanks to good theology! Theology should be based on pastoral work, just as pastoral work should be supported by good theology and not be disconnected from it. And in the spiritual life meeting people nourishes prayer, and in its turn prayer drives us to go out to people. That circular path between theology, pastoral work, and prayer should become the story of one's life.

From the intellectual and spiritual point of view, what did your time spent in Washington give you?

In the United States I discovered the influence that Ignatian spirituality had on my life. For daily decisions about what to do or not do, the help of Ignatian discernment was vital. And in fact, during the first three years that I was rector at Imus I led the seminarians using St. Ignatius's method. Discernment is necessary not only in your personal life but also for your studies.

Which writers made the most impression on you during your studies in America?

The French Dominican Yves Congar, the German Jesuit Karl Rahner, Cardinal Joseph Ratzinger. And as well as these, Hervé Marie Legrand and Jean-Marie Tillard among contemporaries and St. Augustine from among the church fathers. In America during those years I followed the writings of Avery Dulles, Joseph Komonchak, David Tracy, and David Noel Power, an Oblate monk, who specialized in liturgical studies.

Among the South Americans I read a lot of Leonardo Boff, Gustavo Gutiérrez, and Segundo Galilea. Among the women, I read Professors Elizabeth Johnson, Elisabeth Schüssler Fiorenza, and Rosemary Ruether. Among the Asians I read Michael Amaladoss, José de Mesa, a Filipino layman, my ex-professor Catalino Arevalo, doyen of Asian theologians, as well as Aloysius Pieris and Joseph Smith. Among the Italians I read many lectures by Cardinal Carlo Maria Martini. Reading him helped me greatly in my preaching of the spiritual exercises. I only met him once, at a meeting of the Paul VI Institute while he was archbishop of Milan. I was also interested in the theological approach of Severino Dianich and Bruno Forte.

Yes, I have to admit that I have had a rather eclectic education. In addition, if I am considering the benefits of my period in America I can count the scientific rigor of theological study, which helped to train my mind, particularly in methodology. I greatly appreciate the way of doing theology in the United States because it is very attentive to method. Komonchak, my professor for my doctorate, was a disciple of Bernard Lonergan, a Jesuit who published an important book titled *Method in Theology*. I also absorbed this way of reasoning for matters of everyday life.

What relationship did you have with American culture?

During my first years as a student in Washington I felt like an outsider, a stranger. But then, my attitude changed as my personal contacts changed. Through relating to other people I began to get into American culture, and I learned such a lot. For culture is not a randomly organized structure; you have to get into it through people. The concept of culture is an abstraction. In order to experience and get to know it properly, you have to meet someone or several people or a family who enable you to live it. Take an example: the sense of justice and responsibility for others, which is very strong among Americans. When I discovered that I was unable to pay for my university board and lodging, my professor, Father Komonchak, was very embarrassed. He said to me: "I'll take you on as my assistant, so I can pay you something each month and you'll be able to pay for your board and lodging." That little conversation revealed to me the typically American sense of justice I was talking about.

After you left, you went home.

On February 27, 1992, I celebrated the tenth anniversary of my ordination as a priest. On the following day, the

dean of the faculty of theology at Catholic University said
to me, that since I had become a doctor of sacred theology, I could telephone my bishop to tell him so. On the
evening of February 28, I phoned the Philippines (where
it was already the 29th), and I heard that that very day
Bishop Perez had died of a heart attack. It was a shock!
Almost at once, I asked myself, "So what shall I do?" The
apostolic administrator of the diocese made me return
home, because they needed a rector of the seminary. So, in
May 1992, I re-entered the country and began my service
as rector of the major seminary in Tagaytay. At the same
time I taught theology with the Verbites and the Jesuits,
as well as with the Scheut Missionaries. In the mornings I
taught in Manila; in the afternoon at the Jesuits, and in the
evening I returned to Imus.

A very busy life and also rather a complicated one.

Indeed! At that period the Filipino Bishops' Conference
also asked me for various kinds of help, for example, with
the commission for the doctrine of the faith, preaching the
spiritual exercises to bishops, monks, and various congre-
gations. In 1995 I also began working for the Federation
of Asian Bishops' Conferences (FABC) on the occasion of
the visit of John Paul II to Manila for World Youth Day.
On that occasion, for the plenary meeting of the bishop
delegates from the whole of Asia, I gave my first lecture
to the FABC bishops. And a joke was played on me. I was
told that Pope John Paul II had also been there listening
to me. "Church in Asia in the Service of Life and for the

Poor" was the title of my talk. When I finished I almost "ran" out of the room because I was scared of the bishops' reactions and comments.

In the refectory during the coffee break, a Vietnamese bishop came up to me. He reassured me, saying, "Come with me." He was Monsignor François Xavier Thuan, who until recently had been bishop of Saigon. He had been detained in prison for thirteen years and then under house arrest. He told me about his life. We began talking at four in the afternoon and finished at eleven o'clock at night. At the end of our talk he said to me, "From now on call me uncle! And anytime you come to Rome, come and visit me." And so it has been. We have kept up a strong friendship. To me he is a saint. I know that the beatification process has begun. I was not summoned to the hearing, but I want to send my testimony. When I went to visit him in Rome, if he had time he took me to a Chinese or Italian restaurant. But he didn't eat. One day we had supper in his apartment in Piazza San Callisito, a piece of Asia in Trastevere; there were Asian decorations, ornaments, and vestments. In 2002 I went to Rome for the course for newly appointed bishops, since I had been ordained the previous year. He had died a few days before, and I was able to go to his funeral.

Let's go back to Imus. How did you get on with your work as a priest?

After my return from the United States I was very busy, as I said before, with various jobs. First of all as rector of the seminary. So I wrote a directory for seminaries and the first draft of the protocol for procedure in cases of abuse committed by clergy. I received many invitations from different people to give lectures. When I had time and opportunity, I still tried to work as a priest side by side with the poor. And I also tried to keep close to them by my lifestyle, for example, by not having a car but using public transportation. I only began using a mobile phone when I was appointed bishop.

How did you get on with your work as a seminary teacher?

I was inspired by the model I had seen in action in the United States: person to person teaching. Apart from lectures, one-on-one meetings are the most educational. I used to tell the seminarians: I am very busy but as your rector I am here for you, not just for the formal things, but first and foremost to meet each other. And indeed, I ate with them, I cleaned my own room (without the help of the cleaning women). I went on foot or by public transportation just as they did. Students could knock at my door at any time because they knew I was always available for them.

What is the most important thing in the education of a priest?

Education is a total process. But in my experience purifying your motives depends on being truthful about yourself. Does a candidate know himself well or is he hiding from himself? It is a battle to be fought, but together, with patience, you get to the truth. You have to give young people confidence, make them feel we are with them on the journey. Truth and freedom: these two words seem fundamental to me because training is a process. Being with young people on their journey needs patience. The teacher must not be an administrator but a fellow traveler. I wept with them and smiled with them. A little while ago, an ex-seminarian said to me: "Your Eminence, you were my kindest teacher, but I also realized that you were the most demanding. I was always under your shadow." I did not want the seminarians to obey an external law, but that they should internalize it. Also because later in the parish it will be the priest who leads the flock, not the bishop.

The years go by and in 1997 you were appointed to the International Theological Commission.

When the Prefect Joseph Ratzinger introduced me to Wojtyła, he told him that I was the youngest member of the commission. And he asked me how old I was. I said, "Forty." He said: "I thought you were twenty!" When we had to line up for the photograph of all the members, Ratzinger called me to him again to put me beside John Paul II. He asked me my age and then asked, "Have you already made your first communion?" And in later years when we met he teased me with the same joke. In fact, at the cardinals' last audience with Pope Benedict, before his resignation, a cardinal came up to me and said,

"Cardinal Tagle, don't cry!" Then I thought: "Now I'll make Benedict laugh." When he greeted us one by one, I thanked him for his pontificate and told him that the Filipino church was very grateful. Then I whispered in his year, "And, Your Holiness, I *have* made my first communion." He laughed. When the journalists asked me what I had said to the pope to make him laugh, I replied, "Papal secret!"

From 1997 until 2003 you were a member of the International Theological Commission, that is, you belonged to the "aristocracy" of official Catholic theological thinking. The president was the "Panzer-Kardinal" Ratzinger. What do you remember about this period?

My involvement with the Theological Commission was like going back to school. I was with people who had written the books that had been used in my training: Bruno Forte, Hermann Pottmeyer, George Cottier, and Albert Vanhoye. At first I was rather afraid, but I was made welcome, even though I was the youngest. They were all much older than me; they could have been my uncles. I learned a lot, not just from the contents of the work but from the actual proceedings of the commission. It was a little lesson in collegiality and communion. The commission meets once a year for a week. But there are various subcommissions. I was appointed to the one on the permanent diaconate, where I met the present Cardinal Gerhard Ludwig Müller. From our subcommission, six members were later made bishops. To prepare the document on the permanent diaconate we divided the work into groups. My job was to study the development of the discussion on this ministry during the Second Vatican Council. I presented my work, and Cardinal Ratzinger thanked me because, as he said, I had turned a not very interesting topic into something exciting. A comment that gratified me. I have kept in contact with some of those who were members of the commission then: with Monsignor Bruno Forte; with the archbishop of Digione, Roland Minnerath; with the archbishop of Utrecht, Cardinal Willem Jacobus Eijk, whose diocese is twinned with a diocese in the Philippines; with Professor Pottmeyer of Münster.

Finally, if you had to list the three essential gifts of a good theologian, what would you say?

There are a number of important characteristics that a theologian should have. The three that I will mention are not the only ones necessary and probably not even the most important: first of all, a deep faith in God. A theologian must believe that God was victorious in Jesus Christ and that the Holy Spirit continues to lead the world to God. Without that faith, a theologian cannot explain why the gospel really is good news. Theology must not obscure God or God's great works.

Second, a theologian must have in him a great love for people, love for the poor, and love for the world. That love leads the theologian to take people seriously, their cultures and their histories. All this ensures that the theologian believes in the God who is present and speaks through people. That requires a theologian to have a direct and constant presence in people's lives and concerns.

Lastly, a theologian must have a certain sense of humor. A theologian, man or woman, must work hard but must not think that his or her learned work is the last word on anything. A theologian without humor produces arid, lifeless theology. A sense of humor allows you to let go in God.

5

Manila, Philippines

Manila, the capital of Asia's most Catholic country, has 14 million inhabitants. Since 2011 Cardinal Luis Antonio Gokim Tagle has been archbishop of Manila. Legally, his archdiocese has had "only" 3 million people (80 percent Catholic), since a few years ago the huge diocese was subdivided into several smaller ones. But it's clear that Tagle is "the" pastor of Manila, the reference point for the metropolis and the whole church in that area.

In the pages that follow he himself explains well what it means to be bishop of such an enormous and complex urban area. First and foremost, these pages reveal, with disarming simplicity, his awareness of the huge range of human, social, and spiritual challenges at stake, and at the same time, his certainty that the only really important thing is witness to Christ. "A bishop does not have all the solutions to people's problems," the Cardinal candidly admits, "but like Peter and John in the Acts of the Apostles I also say, 'I have no gold or silver but what I have I give you: in the name of Jesus Christ of Nazareth, rise and walk!'"

In his diocese Tagle deals daily with the problem of pastoral structures and the urgent need for adequate resources to preach the gospel. But over time he has developed a solid conviction: "The church does not lack human spaces: only the opportuni-

*ties to preach the gospel," independently of the human and eco-
nomic resources at its disposal. It is enough to read the reality
in the light of the Word. "As a pastor I am aware that I must
proclaim the Good News, not just the Good News as it is written down but Good News that people can experience." There
is a "fifth gospel," we might say, paraphrasing Tagle's words,
which is being written silently day by day by so many anonymous believers. And we need to bring that to light.*

*Furthermore, faced with the typical anonymity of a big city,
Tagle explains, "The pastoral method we have picked is to set
up small Christian base communities, for example, consisting
of families who live in the same street." A simple but practical
answer for a faith that is shared and lived by.*

*Being a pastor in a city like Manila, a capital suffering from
the enormous problem of corruption and waste of public money,
may mean that you must raise your voice in the name of the
gospel, in defense of the people and the rights of the poor. But
never merely denouncing. "Yes, it's true," says the Cardinal,
that the church shares some common ideals with many organizations and some politicians. But we must ensure that our
response is clearly inspired by the gospel and the church's social
teaching, not by ideologies or the desire to compete for power."*

From Imus to Manila. Tell us.

Before I got to Manila I was bishop in Imus, which lies
south of Manila and is a suffragan diocese of it. Today

Imus is becoming part of Metro-Manila,[1] together with two other neighboring cities. So when I was there, I also had the experience of pastoral work in a big city, in contact with migrants, poor people, and people seeking work. I have been archbishop of Manila since 2011. The archdiocese has 3 million inhabitants, 80 percent Catholic, but Metro-Manila has 14 million. Thank God, eleven years ago it was divided up, and six new dioceses were created.

You are pastor of a huge, densely populated metropolis, where there seems to be hardly any available space left. But you like to say that rather than working on "territorial" spaces, the church should work on "human spaces." What does that mean?

A very obvious phenomenon in a great metropolis is that the church lacks territorial spaces for building new churches, pastoral centers, schools, gardens: no room! Thus we have discovered that the most important space in the task of preaching the gospel is the human space, that is, people's daily lives, as *Gaudium et Spes* puts it: "The joy and hope, the grief and distress of people today, especially the poor and those who are suffering, are also the joy and hope, the grief and distress of the disciples of Christ." This is the proper place to preach

---

1. Metropolitan Manila (Kalakhang Maynila in Filipino) is the "national capital region" of the Philippines, consisting of sixteen cities and one municipality.

the gospel, as John Paul II confirmed when he said that the way of the church is the same way that Jesus went, the human way.[2]

In my experience the church does not lack human spaces: there are so many opportunities to preach the gospel, in both senses, bringing the gospel into people's lives, but also discovering the presence of the Spirit of the Lord in daily life. It is not just the church bringing Jesus to people, because Jesus is already present there. That is a very important aspect of mission work, which we tend to forget. The church is a reality that points to a presence, the presence of God, but the church does not create that presence; it's there already! The church is called to make people aware of that presence.

This is a very important idea in Jesuit spirituality and for Pope Francis himself, which he keeps repeating, that before us, the missionaries, the church, God has already made himself present everywhere in the world, and so "his presence does not have to be brought about, but discovered, revealed."[3]

Yes, that is a salient idea in the spiritual vision of Ignatius himself and has to do with seeing, loving, and serving

---

2. *Centesimus annus,* no. 62: "Also in the third millennium the church will be faithful in making the human way her own, in the awareness that she does not go on her way alone but with Christ, her Lord. It is he who made the human way his own and he leads even when people do not realize it."

3. *Evangelii gaudium,* no. 71.

God in all things. A missionary who follows this vision with conviction does not claim to be the only messenger of the gospel. Every missionary is also taught the gospel by the Spirit of Jesus, which he or she as a missionary meets where they are carrying out their mission. After all, the Holy Spirit is the main agent of the church's missionary activity.

I know some people who use this vision to maintain that there is no need of the church or missionary work, because God's Spirit is present everywhere. Someone saying this ignores the central question of what mission is. In order to explain it let's go back to family experience. Yes, every day, every moment, and every action in families display love and attachment. But they also have to celebrate wedding anniversaries, birthdays, and holidays; they have to recall the joys and sorrows in the lives of grandparents; they have to dry the tears of those who are sick or close to death. Without these "signs" of love, what is usually called "omnipresent love" will vanish from the consciousness of those who say they have it.

Nevertheless—you admit it yourself—it is difficult in a metropolis like Manila not to feel overwhelmed by such a complex city.

Yes, that has happened to me sometimes. I have quite often felt overwhelmed by so many problems. I've felt almost impotent, but that impotence in the face of the challenges and the mass of humanity living in the city has taught me to be humble. A bishop does not have all the solutions to people's problems. But like Peter and John in the Acts of the Apostles I also say, "I have no gold or silver but what I have I give you: in the name of Jesus Christ of Nazareth, rise and walk!"

Humility means that your only wealth is the name of the Lord. Often, when poor people present me with questions and dilemmas, I humbly reply, "Look, I'm confused too; I haven't got the answers, because like you I feel very limited, and I too ask why about certain situations." This is a precious lesson for me. Pastoral work in a large urban metropolis like Manila has pressed me into solidarity with people in our common suffering, and made me realize the lack of human wisdom to find adequate solutions to terrible problems. In other words, the bishop needs help just like anyone else.

Where and on what occasions does the archbishop of Manila physically meet the poor?

This often happens at festivals in the parishes, when there are celebrations. After Mass there is lunch with the people, and we tell each other what is going on in a very informal context. But there are also meetings organized with specific groups of poor people, such as those who have no land to cultivate, those who are evicted from their homes, those who lose their jobs, indigenous groups who come from outside Manila to ask the church to intercede for them with some government departments. Then I have begun to go each month to an area where there are many poor people, even if it is not for a particular feast, but just to see the situation, meet people and listen to what the poor have to say about their lives.

I have to say that this encounter with the massive poverty endured in their daily lives by so many is not easy. Then I also have to present the requests of the poor to institutions. Recently, for example, I went to ask for houses for children who were sick and suffering from malnutrition. On that occasion I talked to the children and heard the families' stories. Still on the subject of children: there is a house in Manila for street girls, which was also visited by Pope Francis. These visits are tricky; obviously we have to respect their trust but they are deep encounters. And again, when I go by car to the airport very early in the morning (at three o'clock) I see homeless families. And I always feel upset and disturbed when toward five in the morning I see the police make the poor people who have slept on the ground get up, so that the gardens can be tidied up. By day people are not aware of this, but when it is dark you see the reality.

How do you react to such sights?

Seeing those scenes has made me lose hours of sleep; those images stick in my mind. The poor also appear in my speeches. When the opportunity arises, in homilies or in meetings with priests, I talk about what I have seen. In short, the lack of physical spaces forces us to rely less on structures and more on life sharing. Of course, we also have to have a well-organized response to people's needs, but I try to maintain the balance between informal human contact and structured initiatives. Human contact without a practical response becomes sentimentalism, but an aid structure without human contact deteriorates into bureaucracy. I don't want the church's mission work to be compared to bureaucratic activity, because it is a mission that has its roots in the Lord's love. Pope Francis himself also reminded us: "The church is not an NGO [non-governmental organization]." It's a real temptation. As the church of Manila we can't not network with other Christian churches, and adherents of other religions, NGOs, and organized groups for the poor. We can't do everything on our own. But I think it important that the church's identity should be quite clear.

How does the Diocese of Manila link in practice with people in these "human spaces"? Can you give some examples?

Well, there are so many, and the bishop can't embrace them all. So I delegate to others, in particular to lay people, as well as to auxiliary bishops. The former not only have hearts full of love but also have competence. For example, in the financial sphere, for the dialogue between the world of business and the poor we have set up a conference of Catholic bishops and businessmen who meet twice a year; and every month they have a discussion on a particular subject. In the last two years, the job has been inclusive development, because most people—even though general well-being is improving—are in fact excluded from development. Into this "human space" the church brings the voice of the poor. I have taken part in so many meetings of this group and each time, among the speakers, there were two poor people among the men in suits and ties. Yes, because we not only need statistics but also life stories. When the businessmen and entrepreneurs invite me, if I can spare the time I go, because the "human space" is not easy to open, but when there is an opportunity I take it.

And the results come, slowly, slowly. For example, every businessman has to exercise corporate social responsibility (CSR). But in order to put this into practice, it is necessary to hear about people's everyday lives. Without knowing about actual situations businessmen have no contact with reality, and it remains just theory. So, for example, in one of those meetings a community of poor people says, "We have no drinking water," and a representative of the business world undertakes to deal with that.

Another particular example: through Caritas so many societies contribute to scholarships for children who otherwise could not afford to study; now we have about 1,500 students. Another result: after "chewing over" the church's social doctrine, some of these people involved in the business world become lay spokespeople for that doctrine. And this is important, because they put their skills as lay people to good effect and stand in for priests in speaking about social problems.

As pastor of this diocese, do you feel Manila is more like Jerusalem, capital of the faith, or Nineveh, a "pagan" city in need of conversion?

In every believer there is an unbeliever. That is true not only for individuals but also for communities. We do not act wholly in accordance with the faith at every moment. In that sense faith and unbelief go together, so I can answer that Manila (like other cities and places) is at the same time a bit like Jerusalem and a bit like Nineveh. For me the presence of the "unbeliever" in us is the reason for our inconsistency in the way we live by our faith. That inconsistency represents a challenge to deepen our faith, growing closer to Jesus Christ. As a pastor, I am conscious that I must proclaim the Good News, not just the Good News as it is written but as it is experienced in people's lives, thus to encourage the faithful, showing them God's grace, which has enabled us to live according to the gospel and thank the Father for that. Discovering the presence of the gospel in people's lives is decisive. But the Good News is also a criticism, a call to conversion and to a life more in accordance with the faith we profess.

So, first you have to make people realize that they are loved and then call them to conversion.

We have had confirmation of the value of this pastoral approach from a recent poll carried out among teenagers by the diocesan Youth Commission. One of the most interesting results is that when church leaders speak like angry politicians rather than as loving pastors, young people no longer want to listen to them. So the pastor can and should give criticism, not angrily but in a spirit of love and understanding.

That response to the poll by the young people confirms an intuition I have had for many years. In a metropolis people are anonymous; so many feel like ghosts. For young people a sense of belonging is very important (anonymity is a deep wound), so they must find a home in the church, and see the pastor as a father ready to welcome them.

That cannot always be expressed by physical presence. But, thank God, we have the mass media that can help us: TV and radio, Facebook, YouTube. In my case these allow me to contact so many people who watch the Sunday broadcast of the liturgy of the Word, thus giving me a space in their lives every Sunday!

Is that a common reflection on urban pastoral work for FABC, the Asian Bishops' conferences?

In the great cities of Asia the pastoral method we have developed is the setting up of small Christian base communities (CBC), consisting, for example, of families living on the same street, because this is a response to anonymity. The same goes also for very remote rural zones, where the distances are great and the priest cannot get there every Sunday. The CBCs make it possible for people to be looked after more fully and give visibility to the image of the church, beloved in Africa, as "God's family."

You insist on stressing that "the poor are the best teachers, even in the faith." Can you explain this sentence better? Are the poor nearer to God? Why?

If I think about the Filipino situation, the poor live every day with a lack of prospects, uncertainty; they don't know where to go; they are not sure anyone will listen to them properly (for example, the public authorities). Once a woman said to me, "It's easy to say, 'Give us this day our daily bread,' when you are sure that you will have a meal waiting for you. But when we get home there is no bread. And yet, we continue to pray." Well, that's a painful prayer, of pure faith. Because there is no certainty that her prayer will be heard. So I consider that woman to be a teacher of faith!

The risk for us is to pray in a rhetorical way, whereas that woman has taught me that so many people pray with tears! And God—alone—surely hears her in order to answer her in his own time and according to his mysterious ways. Like Job, the poor teach me to accept what happens. That's why I agree with Pope Francis: we need to go to the margins, to the "human spaces," not only to teach but also to learn the Good News.

By saying that, aren't you afraid of being accused of "pauperism"? The rich could reproach the church for forgetting about them.

The attention the church and society should pay to the poor does not mean forgetting the others. The truth is that when we go to the poor we go out to all. This is also a temptation for me: when I am the guest of a rich family or go to parties given by people who are well off, I find a lot of generosity, but there's the risk that my attention is not focused on the people but on the donations they can give me. But when I go to the poor I only see their bare humanity. And for me this is a great lesson in purification: when I go out to the bare humanity of the poor, my love for the rich also becomes purified. I always invite my rich friends to have human contact with the poor to enrich themselves in humanity.

When I was rector at Tagaytay, every year there was a day for thanking the benefactors of the seminary. A point came when we decided that that day should also be an occasion for Christian and human education. I always included an appeal to the rich: don't just help the seminary but also (above all) the poor people in their parishes. Jokingly, but not altogether, I told these benefactors: "If you don't help the poor, I won't accept your donations to the seminary." I repeat the same thing to volunteers in the parishes: to readers at Mass I say, "You proclaim God's word, but after Mass I encourage you to go to the poor to proclaim it there too, not just within the cathedral walls."

Perhaps the poor are closer to God because they experience the dimension of precariousness "structurally" and so they are less tied to material goods.

The Bible says clearly, and I can attest to that in human experience, that the poor are closer to God not because they are better or holier than others. No. The poor are sinners just like the rest of humanity. But the poor are close to God, or rather, God has a special love for them, because they need God. Often they have no one else to cling to. From that situation, the poor receive a wisdom that can only come from God as a gift of grace.

Another precious lesson received from the poor is the strength of the human spirit. They are accustomed to disasters, whether these are natural disasters or life's adversities. Every day is a disaster for them: they lack food, they lack the opportunity to study and to look after themselves. For them life is a disaster, but it is a mystery of grace to see how these people are able to deny themselves, to think of others, to smile. For example, after a typhoon, when the sun comes out again, it's enough to make them happy again. For us the sun rises every day, but we do not appreciate this gift.

Here's another example. Once a seminarian whom I had sent to a remote community of indigenous people —"primitive" in general parlance—gave me precious reports of that community about the lessons of kindness he had learned from them (they live in the southwest of the island of Luzon). Once, he told me, it did not rain for two weeks. The whole community, consisting of about a hundred families, was affected. One day the family with whom the seminarian was staying went hunting and caught a wild boar. The seminarian (who had grown up with the pragmatic mentality of the city) suggested: if we cut it up into pieces, we can eat it over two weeks. But his host replied, "This is not a gift just for our family; it's for the whole community. I could not eat happily if I knew that others had nothing to eat: we must share it. Tomorrow we will all be hungry again, but we are all the same."

For me that was an important lesson. Poverty does not become a reason for being selfish, but an opportunity to share. I don't want to canonize the poor, but there is this dimension, and it is a sign of the Lord's presence.

There are still many poor people in the Philippines, but consumerism is also spreading. In the cities commercial centers are sprouting up like mushrooms. Are you in favor of Masses in shopping centers or not?

Oases of prayer in commercial centers and also in business offices or banks can act as a "conscience" in the world of consumerism. Without these oases, that world would be purely consumerist and materialist. In that desert, dominated by money and profit, it is an oasis where we can remember the transcendent dimension and not think only about our individual interest. But it must be an area dedicated to prayer that has its own dignity. The celebrations held there must follow all the liturgical rules. And they must not be ways of making money but opportunities for mission. In a certain sense chapels in commercial centers are "mission centers." The people's offerings go to poor parishes, for projects to help the hungry, for catechesis, charitable programs. In shops people buy for themselves, but in these chapels they offer money for others.

The Philippines is a very Catholic country, it is said. Nevertheless, it always struggles to find political figures who are able to cope with the situation. Indeed, often the political class is guilty of favoritism and corruption. In August 2014 you too went to the square with 350 thousand people to denounce the "pork barrel system."[4] Why is it so difficult to "evangelize politics"?

For a start, unlike with Christian faith or morality, politics is an example of what I said before about the presence of an "unbeliever" in every believer. But history also plays an important part in the type of politics we have today. Unfortunately, the "ruling class" model is still deeply rooted in our society. The leaders are masters, and the people simply followers. In fact we still have not gotten a fully democratic government where it really is the people who decide. Of course, in the Constitution we find high-flown words about democracy and people power, but it is different in practice. The politicians behave like father-masters, and the people

---

4. This is the name given to the practice of quite a few politicians of spending public money to finance projects in their own electoral constituencies.

wait patiently to be helped. Naturally the political class does not want to change this mentality, because the benefits they give become the object of blackmail, gratitude becomes servility. This cultural scenario is deeply entrenched and very difficult to change. Formal changes are not enough; we need a change of heart. Clearly a system like that is open to corruption. For ordinary citizens it is enough that their needs are attended to. Everything else—the common good—does not count or comes later. The political system is more susceptible to dishonest and manipulative practices because it is not devoted to service, especially of the poor.

What is the church doing to change things?

With the help of various NGOs and grass-roots organizations the level of political awareness is rising. But there is still a long way to go. At the moment we are shaken because last year the revelations in the media about the phenomenon of political corruption revealed a situation that was unimaginable in its vastness and ramifications. Hence the important public demonstrations that were organized. The shock opened people's eyes. The investigations continue, and that is positive. Whereas they used to be untouchable, today many senators have been brought to court, with the possibility of being condemned and losing their privileges. The church is one of the voices raised against such corruption. But I am always cautious on this front, because I don't want the church to be con-

fused with the NGOs. And public opinion has understood that.

In what way?

I can explain by means of something that happened. In
mid-2013, on the day we held a press conference to present our conference on the New Evangelization, at the end
a journalist asked me my opinion on what was coming out
from the investigations. "I have no words to describe my
feelings," I said. "I am very surprised by how widespread
the matter is. I wonder, Have these politicians ever visited
the houses of the poor? Have they touched the hands of
suffering people? Are the poor present in their minds?
When people of good will meet a poor person, their minds
open and their hearts do not want to rob them." While I
was speaking, my voice cracked. I couldn't go on speaking,
tears poured down my cheeks. That same afternoon the
picture of me in tears went out on TV. There it is. I think
that the image of a pastor weeping over the poor because of
the injustice they suffer was my contribution to the cause,
not just denunciations! Yes, it's true that the church shares
common ideals with many organizations and a few politicians. We have to make sure that our response is clearly
inspired by the gospel and the church's social doctrine, not
by ideologies or the desire to compete for power.

*A consistent number of Filipino adults, both men and women,
emigrate from the country in search of work. Often these people*

become preachers of the gospel. Can you say anything about that?

When I was a student in the United States for seven years I had the experience of being an immigrant. I learned what it means to live in a culture that is different from your own, eat different food. . . . That stage of my life taught me important lessons: I saw the contribution of the Filipino community to the church's life in Washington and, in general, in the United States. I always have these experiences in mind that I gained during my stay in the States.

As a pastor today, I travel a lot everywhere, and I see the situation of Filipino and other migrants. In many meetings and gatherings I have the opportunity to talk about this, but also to listen to the testimonies of people from various parts of the world in contact with Filipino communities. I am thinking about a Jordanian nun I met recently, a Swiss bishop from Arabia, the Capuchin friar Paul Hinder, Cardinals Giuseppe Betori from Florence and Angelo Scola of Milan. . . . I learned about the situation of Filipinos in a good many countries. An Iraqi bishop asked me, "Why do they leave their country and come to Iraq? They are good Christians, but why do they leave their families?" That question struck me. The reason is poverty. Having said that, I can add that so many bishops tell me that it is because of the Filipino migrants that the churches remain open and full and the number of Sunday Masses has increased.

Here is an example of the paschal mystery: there is the cross and death but in that death something positive remains: the faith that rises again in countries in need of this Christian presence. That reminds me of the bit in the Creed that says, "He descended into hell." When he was dead Jesus shared the death and suffering of the people in the world of the dead. With him they rise to new life. The Filipino migrants go to various countries throughout the world as crucified people; they too, one could say, are dead, far as they are from their families. But by doing this, without fully realizing it, they become instruments for the resurrection of the faith. But we must not be blind to the sufferings and abuses that many Filipino migrants suffer personally. Their contribution to Christian communities in the countries they go to live in must never be an excuse to tolerate the exploitation they endure.

All that is a big responsibility for the migrants.

Yes, but also for us Filipino bishops, because we have to ask ourselves how best to prepare those who emigrate. That preparation has to take place in daily life, in liturgy, and catechism. Personally, when I was the parish priest in Imus cathedral, in order to offer a minimum of preparation, I tried to gather people together who were about to go abroad. But it is difficult also because in many of the places they go to it is not easy to say you are Catholic. I conclude by adding that various Filipino dioceses have a ministry for migrants that aims to help the families and those who stay behind, especially children, to overcome the psychological shock of being parted from their loved ones.

As well as to families, emigration brings in money to the coffers of the Filipino state, which regards the migrants as "new heroes," but it has a very high social cost. What position does the church take toward this phenomenon?

As I said, the phenomenon of mass emigration from the Philippines has its roots in so many people's poverty. It is a crying shame that the country does not offer enough jobs and that many Filipinos have to seek work outside their country, often very far from home. Migration represents a failure of the society, of the political class, and the business world. The church stresses this strongly.

People have the right to migrate. Unfortunately many are forced to migrate because of poverty. And then they have to give money to the government and send money home to their families for their basic needs. So it all becomes very expensive for them. The children grow up with one parent or even both parents absent. Marital fidelity is strained. Consequently the church develops programs to help and give positive answers to these dire effect of migration. In the Philippines we try to provide spiritual support, including emotional support, to the wives and children who are left behind by their husbands or fathers. And as well as that, we teach them how to spend the money wisely that they get from abroad.

The Filipino bishops' conference also co-ordinates with the local churches where there are large communities of Filipino immigrants. Where necessary, we send Filipino bishops, nuns, and monks or lay missionaries to look after their various needs, including legal questions and to help them integrate into the new societies they are living in.

6

Asia Today and Tomorrow

The continent from which Cardinal Luis Antonio Gokim Tagle comes is the least Christian continent in the world, if we take account of the number of baptized. Nevertheless, it is a continent where that "little flock" which is the Catholic Church manifests a witness to the faith that has a lot to say to the other churches, including those with a long tradition, such as the Western churches. "In countries where Christians are a minority, the church is respected, because of the educational institutions, hospitals, and social services it runs. People realize that Christians are a small community that contributes to the common good, even beyond its own people. Not all become Christians, of course, but many appreciate that opportunity."

Like other continents in the world, today Asia is strongly affected by the phenomenon of globalization: at the heart of its capital cities the biggest and brightest commercial centers in the world are sprouting up. Aware of this, Cardinal Tagle neither gives way to anachronistic nostalgia nor blindly follows the call of modernity and its sirens. "It's not possible to stop the phenomenon of globalization," he explains. "However, the church must teach people how to engage in self-criticism and discernment. We need to overcome the temptation to go indiscriminately for the 'new' and what comes from 'abroad' and not value our own identity. Besides, let us not forget that with globalization comes the risk of exclusion even of God from society's view!"

His plan is clear: the challenge is to humanize globalization. And in order to do so, "the church must first of all point to a 'globalization of values' accepted by all nations: truth, love, human life. . . . Here interreligious and ecumenical dialogue is very important."

For Tagle, dialogue with the great religions is a top priority (he practices it in Manila) and also very difficult to do, especially in the light of the extremely delicate international geopolitical context. "There remains the great challenge of fundamentalism; it has come into politics and ruined the sense of dialogue."

Asia is the continent where Jesus Christ came from, although in numbers, it is the least Christianized. Looking to the future, are you optimistic about the proclamation of the gospel on this continent?

Yes, because—despite so many problems—in Asia we are seeing an increase in baptisms, and also in seminarians, monks, and nuns. The numbers are small in relation to the total population of Asia, but significant. In countries where Christians are a minority, the church is respected, because of the educational institutions, hospitals, and social services it runs. People realize that Christians are a small community that contributes to the common good, even beyond its own people. Not all become Christians, of course, but many appreciate that opportunity. In Kuala Lumpur, the capital of Malaysia, I have met government officials who have openly expressed to me their appreciation for the education they received from Catholic schools. Even years later they remain friends with the priests and nuns who were their teachers. At Malpensa airport in Milan, a Chinese lady from Hong Kong told me she had studied in a Catholic school. And in her turn she had sent her children and grandchildren to Catholic schools because she appreciates the sense of discipline and values that the church communicates in them. And that lady was a Buddhist.

Since the publication of the declaration Dominus Iesus *in 2000, interreligious dialogue in Asia seems to be marking time. How to proceed with this?*

In fact, during these years interreligious dialogue, both at base level and at that of the FABC (Federation of Asian Bishops' Conferences), has continued without a break. In some areas of Asia it has even broadened, involving bishops and imams. For example, this happens on the island of Mindanao. Here too in Manila we have interreligious meetings—every month whenever possible and on the more important occasions—with Buddhists, Muslims, and representatives of other religions. Of course, there remains the great challenge of fundamentalism, which has entered politics and ruined the sense of dialogue. Politicians use religion to gain approval. However, positive signs are not lacking.

For years the Philippines has also experienced the challenge of Islamic fundamentalism; you only have to see what happened in Mindanao. Will you give us your reading of the situation?

For many years the various administrations of the Filipino government have had to face the complex question of Mindanao. Some mostly Islamic regions of that island want to separate from the central government in Manila, whereas other areas don't, but want to remain within the Republic of the Philippines with a certain level of autonomy. The Islamic fundamentalist groups in the Philippines are not easy to describe. Some trustworthy sources say that some of these groups were initially trained by the army and the secret services to combat the left-wing military groups or communist elements, but that now they are in conflict with the government. Other trustworthy sources say that these groups are no longer inspired by an ideology as they were in the past. At present all they want is to get money by kidnapping people and demanding a ransom. There are different factions within the Muslim groups seeking autonomy or independence. When the government begins a peace process with one faction, it is said that other small groups try to sabotage it and stall the process. The situation is more complex than it looks.

In the West we know little about it but there is a "made in Asia" theology, or even theologies (in the plural). How can these contribute to a general reflection on the adaptation ("inculturation") of the gospel to today's context?

It's right to use the plural, because there are as many theologies as there are "cultural worlds" to which they relate. Using the metaphor of food, we could speak of "chopstick Asia" (China, Japan, Korea . . .), "curry Asia" (India, Pakistan, Sri Lanka, Bangladesh . . .), "banana leaf Asia" (Philippines, Indonesia, Malaysia . . .) and so on. Certainly in every Asian country there is a mixture of Asian cultures. In various parts of Asia not only the cultures but also the religions are very different. Just by way of example, Buddhism in India is very different from the Buddhism in Japan or China. Adaptation ("inculturation") of the faith by means of theology is promoted by and in the local churches and, at continental level, by FABC (Federation of Asian Bishops' Conferences), through its office dealing with theological matters.

All this offers a richness: not only do other continents learn from Asia, but we Asians should also learn from other Asian theologies. I myself discovered the depth of Asian cultures and the importance of the influence of Asian religions on different cultures. To give an example, FABC organized a seminar on mixed and interreligious marriages. We listened to couples belonging to different faiths. Every religion has its own understanding of the role of the man and the role of the woman in marriage.

Every religion has its own way of bringing up children. On that occasion I understood how interreligious and intercultural dialogue occurs every day in the homes of these interreligious families and not just in academic circles.

For example, in the case of the Philippines we realized that the local culture has a wisdom that is very close to that of the Bible. It goes without saying that the most important thing in inculturation is to take the actual situation of the people and reflect on the gospel message in that context, not just about the culture in an abstract way. Culture must not be a synonym for something academic but for the mentality, worldview, aspirations, values, shared identity, and belonging that give a sense of security and stability in daily life.

Is there any attempt at inculturation in the liturgy?

I'd like to quote the example of Father Anscar Chupungeo, a Filipino Benedictine, ex-president of the Pontifical Liturgical Institute in Rome, founder of the Paul VI Liturgy Institute, who died in a Mindanao Benedictine monastery. More than twenty years ago he composed the "Filipino People's Mass." He incorporated Filipino elements into it, such as kissing hands and the centrality of the cross. And in that Mass the celebrant is the last to receive communion, because in Filipino culture, when there are guests, the master of the house eats last. So, these rites (still *ad experimentum*) can be used in special circumstances. For example, we used it in the opening celebration of the big conference on the New Evangelization which took place in 2013 in the Philippines. Who knows, perhaps one day we shall celebrate it in Milan with Filipino migrants!

Is there an Asian "liberation theology"?

Yes, in a certain sense, with similarities but also profound differences from Latin American liberation theology. In Asia the theme of liberation is closely linked to the relationship with other religions, not just with poverty. Unfortunately, in Asia politicians and parties often use religion to maintain the status quo, and so the first task for believers in the various religious traditions is to restore religion to its proper role. Through the energies produced by the religions we hope to find a way to liberate from poverty and from the wrong use of religion to divide people. In Asia theological reflection on liberation is also concerned with the sphere of culture, for example, questions like the caste system, which keeps some people trapped in an inferior condition. In that sense we confront situations in which cultures and religious traditions treat women and girls as inferior to men.

If you had to name an Asian—male or female—theologian whom we ought to read in order to understand that Asian sensibility, whom would you suggest?

Among many, I'd like to mention the Jesuits Aloysius Pieris from Sri Lanka and Michael Amaladoss from India.[1] They are well known throughout the world. Then I'd like to mention three other names. First of all, the Sri Lankan Redemptorist Vimal Tirimanna, who focuses on moral theology. He is also a lecturer in a pontifical university in Rome. Second, another Redemptorist, the Filipino Karl Gaspar, who has thought a lot about indigenous populations. Lastly, a Filipino Benedictine nun, Mary John Mananzan, who has studied the ecological question and women's thinking.[2]

In your opinion, what are the most important questions for the church today?

The world seeks a space to encounter Transcendence. The church should be where people who seek the meaning of life are to be found. The "Gentiles' Court" is an example of the kind of initiatives being developed. Taking part in cultural debate is essential, with an attitude that seeks encounter. Here the church needs to learn first of all to be a silent presence and then "a teacher of humanity." There

---

1. Among the books by Aloysius Pieris are *An Asian Theology of Liberation* (Maryknoll, NY: Orbis Books, 1988) and *Love Meets Wisdom: A Christian Experience of Buddhism* (Maryknoll, NY: Orbis Books, 1988). Michael Amaladoss is the author of *The Asian Jesus* (Maryknoll, NY: Orbis Books, 2006) and *Interreligious Encounters* (Maryknoll, NY: Orbis Books, 2017).

2. See *Women Resisting Violence* (Maryknoll, NY: Orbis Books, 1996).

is no human question that is alien to the church. Sometimes she might not have a ready response, but her humble presence is already a sign that the church intends to contribute to the process of human liberation. And since our world is more sensitive to images than to words, we need to learn an appropriate way of communicating from Pope Francis. The church must also confront the profound changes in world cultures and people's vision of reality, especially that of the young. While it must remain faithful to the *kerygma*, the church cannot always just be nostalgic for the "good old days." The world of today will continue to construct its own view of things, whether we like it or not. The church must grasp that and find ways to proclaim that the gospel speaks to *this* world, not just for a world of another age and time.

In Pope Francis's first appearance a lot was made of his presenting himself as "bishop of Rome." He was making a precise theological point. What do you think of it?

There is a widespread tendency to think of the church of Rome as the universal church. The church of Rome is a local church, which of course has a special place in the communion that is the universal church. It represents the church of the martyrs and the witness of the great apostles Peter and Paul. The church of Rome supports the other local churches: at the level of bishops, this is called bishops' collegiality, co-responsibility in the same mission. Pope Francis stresses this point; he wants to breathe new life into collegiality, into listening to other local churches. The more the church of Rome listens to the other churches, the better it fulfills its vocation.

You are one of the authors of the History of Vatican II *published by the "Bologna School." In your opinion what directions of the Council are still failing to be carried out?*

I wrote only one article in the series of volumes comprising the *History of Vatican II*. Knowledge of Vatican II is still incomplete: not even all priests have read all the Council documents. I think that is also true of many monks and nuns, pastoral workers and catechists. That is incomprehensible. Every ecumenical council inaugurates a program for the church and for mission that takes whole generations to be fully understood and carried out. For me Vatican II is a council that has not yet been fully taken on board. That is precisely the task of the church today: to get the hang of it in everyday life, apply the statements of Vatican II to the challenges of the contemporary world. That is why, in my opinion, we don't need a Vatican III. We need to finish studying, understanding, and applying Vatican II. And one of the matters we should give priority to is ecumenical and interreligious dialogue. The peace of the world also depends on the capacity of believers in various religions to live together in an atmosphere of respect.

For us in Asia, the universal church and local churches need to continue assimilating the teaching of Vatican II both in theology and in practice. The FABC has pressed hard for a truly local church in Asia, a church that is truly in communion with the universal church but also truly Asian. We should remember that in many regions of Asia Christianity is still seen as a foreign religion. Just as Europe is seeking to rediscover its Christian roots, we are seeking to rediscover the Asian roots of Christianity!

Now that I am president of Caritas Internationalis and also of the International Biblical Federation, I see how the fundamental directions and vision of Vatican II are valid and can guide us in our responses, both in pastoral and humanitarian work. The Second Vatican Council invites us to concentrate on what we have in common with followers of other religions and to work together to develop society and the common good. On the occasion of the first anniversary of the terrible earthquake in Nepal (April 25, 2015) representatives of the various Caritas organizations from different countries came to Nepal to show their solidarity and put reconstruction programs in place. In the district I visited, situated on mountain slopes, nearly three thousand people died. In the villages I visited, there was not a single Christian. The people welcomed our delegation as if we were kings. They had written songs and poems about their terrible experience, and in all of them they mentioned Caritas. Now the presence of Christians who had shown compassion for all and real caring has become part of their collective memory, and even their folklore. In the short speech I made on that occasion I said, "The earthquake shook the earth and destroyed lives and goods. But the earthquake also shook the hearts of men and women whom you did not know, and their love, our love will help you rebuild your lives and your dreams." But we from Caritas have not the slightest intention of "capitalizing" on their gratitude by inviting them to consider becoming Christians. No. But we witnessed to Christ through love that embraces everybody, especially those in difficulty.

Another important question is about the media: everybody says that preaching the gospel needs to take the media into account, but in practice few local churches have taken that challenge seriously.

That is decidedly true. For years we have been talking about new means of social communication like a new Areopagus, or a new mission area. There has been some progress in the church's involvement in the social media. But we need to do a lot more. The social media are not only tools for preaching the gospel that we need to learn to use in the best way possible. We also need to understand that the social media are a world in themselves, with their own culture, language, methods, priorities, and values. We should not just use the social media to preach the gospel; we must evangelize the world of the social media. If meeting people personally is a way to preach the gospel, then we need to be present in a personal way via the social media. It is not enough to criticize them. We need to take part in them. We can't reach today's young people without the social media. We can take part in the promotion of justice and other noble causes through the social media.

Personally, I have a Sunday broadcast in which I reflect on the biblical readings in the day's Mass. This broadcast is available on YouTube. I have a Facebook page and a Twitter account, which are managed by Jesuit communication experts in Manila. By these means I can be "present" in many houses, in quite a few cars, on mobile phones, and in different countries. I also try to have good relations with people working in the media. On the occasion of Pope Francis's visit to the Philippines in 2015 and the 2016 Eucharistic congress, I held spiritual reflections (including adoration of the Eucharist and confessions) for media workers who had covered these events. I was surprised by the positive response we received.

The penetration of consumerism, a form of globalization, is also highly visible in the Philippines (and in general in Asia). What is your reading of this phenomenon? In your view, with the advent of globalization are people better or worse off than before?

Once again I answer from my own experience. Current globalization is clearly an economic globalization of the neoliberal kind. With regard to the Philippines, through various international economic treaties, our country has been told that it must open its doors to products from all over the world (meat, fruit . . .). From a certain point of view it is positive that people can get products coming in from other parts of the world, but the point is that now our own products do not find other markets. Why? Globalization does not produce equality; its opening up is selective. Some have to open up their markets completely; others can choose. When I was a child I only saw apples and pears at Christmas; today, every day, there is everything. Filipino kids in the big cities no longer see tropical fruit, which ends up in the West at very high prices. It is not up to me to explain the theories, but these are the effects.

Another level is cultural. Other people's values arrive in various contexts. That is a positive thing because horizons are broadened. But again, there is selectivity and inequality. One of the consequences is that globalization leads to the undervaluing of local traditions. Think of film. Every film tells a story but also brings values. This change can be felt! Here the church's global mission comes in. It is not possible to stop the phenomenon of globalization, but still the church should teach people self-criticism and discernment toward the temptations of an indiscriminate openness to the "new" and what comes from "abroad," which ends up devaluing their own identity. Let us not forget that with globalization there comes the risk of exclusion even of God from society's view!

So the church must first of all point to a "globalization of values" accepted by all nations: truth, love, human life. Here interreligious and ecumenical dialogue are very important because they help in the task of humanizing globalization. The problem of globalization is that it must be inclusive, without creating marginalization, as happens today. I also spoke about this at Davos in January 2014. There in Switzerland I took part in a session with various religious leaders who were discussing "How can the world's religions help in the peace process based on respect for human rights?" The interesting thing was to see that the political and economic world had realized that religions have significant forces for challenges of this kind and can make an important contribution.

"The future of the church is in Asia." This saying of Pope Francis caused a stir. You mentioned it.

Saint John Paul II had already said in *Ecclesia in Asia* that the third millennium would see a great harvest for the faith in Asia. Pope Francis repeated this sentence twice to me personally: "The future of the church is in Asia." The first time was when he had just arrived in the Philippines, before he got out of the pope mobile which had taken him from the airport to the Apostolic Nunciature (the seat of the Vatican diplomatic mission). He confided to me, "I saw the enthusiasm of people in Korea, Sri Lanka, the Philippines. There is a future for the church in Asia; the future of the church is in Asia." And he repeated it before he left for Rome. Then I heard he had said the same to priests in Rome, in an assembly in June 2015. And in a longer conversation he explained to me that the church in Asia is small in numbers, but it has so many young people and that makes it an enthusiastic church. Besides, it is a church that endures suffering and martyrdom, from the Middle East to Southeast Asia. Suffering caused by various situations: wars, ethnic conflicts, religious conflicts, typhoons. . . . He himself saw how in the midst of this suffering people profess their Christian faith. That is the church's secret and the pascal mystery: the tomb of death is the tomb of resurrection. I think there are more Christians in Asia than we know of. They are people who believe in Jesus in their hearts, and when there is an opportunity to express or speak of their faith, they will do so.

In Asia vocations are also increasing in significant numbers.

That's true. For example, in Vietnam there are dioceses with two hundred seminarians. In Korea the archdiocese of Seoul has more than two hundred seminarians. Fifty years ago such numbers were unthinkable in these countries and were only to be found in the West. So is there a lack of vocations now? Perhaps not. The vocations are found in other parts of the world. Today the missionaries come from the new churches and help up maintain a sense of community. Years ago, monks from the West came to Asia and Africa to sow the gospel. Now it is time for their children to return the favor to their fathers and mothers in the faith. This is an exchange of grace.

7

Ecology and the Vindication of Laudato Si'

In this last chapter Cardinal Tagle confronts a series of very topical and pressing questions, from world poverty to the problem of the environment. He does so very much in tune with the prophetic thrust of Pope Francis's encyclical Laudato Si'. *At the risk of being called a "communist," as Pope Bergoglio has sometimes been, Tagle strongly reaffirms that humans are the custodians of the created world and not its absolute master and that environmental devastation is caused by human greed.*

Cardinal Tagle is not a recent environmentalist. Even when he was bishop of Imus he already set up a sort of "liturgical season" dedicated to the creation (six weeks from August to October 4, the feast of St. Francis of Assisi), but this initiative did not manage to "break through" within the Filipino church. Now, since the publication of Pope Francis's "green" encyclical, he can claim, without being polemical, to feel himself somewhat "vindicated."

In answering the questions put to him, once again Tagle shows himself capable of weaving together, in an original way, his wisdom and depth as a theologian with his pastoral experience. That pastoral experience has personal contact with poverty and the effects of climate disturbances on the most vulnerable sectors of the population. Indeed, the morning after the Hayan typhoon, which devastated the central area of the Philippines in November 2013, causing millions of deaths and homelessness, Tagle went to the scene and saw in person the dramatic effects on countless poor people, who had become even poorer because of climate change.

He looks at things clearly and passionately. Since being appointed president of Caritas Internationalis, he is a man who, today more than ever, is called upon to help the church measure up in a far-sighted way to the global challenges of today's world.

Pope Francis' encyclical Laudato Si' *marks a change in the papal magisterium, because for the first time it explicitly connects the situation of the poor with the exploitation of "mother Earth." For this Francis has been accused of being a "communist." What do you think of such reactions?*

My first response is existential and comes from my own experience in my country, the Philippines. We know that the first to pay for the consequences of climate change are the poor. The poor are always the most vulnerable people when there is a natural or ecological disaster. I don't claim to enter into the scientific discussions (I am not competent to do so), but for the last forty years our experience in the Philippines has shown us that in these decades we have had more environmental disasters than ever before. For example, when I was a child the highest level for a typhoon was 3. Today the experts have had to add two further levels, and we are now at level 5! My native city, Imus, was not subject to flooding when I was small. But now, with every typhoon the water enters houses or threatens to. This actually happened in my parents' house.

I repeat: I do not take part in the scientific discussions, as I don't feel qualified to do so. But at the same time I have the experience to say that we are facing a deterioration in the environment. In the region of Tacoblan, which I visited after the terrible Hayan typhoon (ten thousand dead) that struck in November 2013, typhoons are fairly frequent. But in this case, although the alert was declared in good time, no preparations were sufficient, given the extreme violence of the typhoon itself. For this reason I welcomed these reflections by the pope very warmly, because I looked from the viewpoint of the poor who suffer most from the environmental damage caused by climate change.

Let's go back to the link between the poor and the environment. As a bishop, a pastor of souls, can you explain to us why these two are linked and go together, as Pope Francis maintains?

Even when I was bishop of Imus I had already set up a sort of "liturgical season" dedicated to the creation: six weeks from August to October 4, the feast of St. Francis of Assisi. Thanks also to the ecological awareness of the Protestant churches and the Orthodox Church, I discovered a spirituality of care for creation and a Christian awareness that sees all creation as one family—an awareness which, we have to admit, is not so strong in the case of the Catholic Church. Nevertheless, we must remember that, according to Christian doctrine, creation is Christocentric: creation is not just by God the Father but also happens in Christ and through Christ. Jesus entered creation as a human person. That opens the door to a deep spirituality of human presence in the world, a call to humanity to be guardians of the created world as collaborators with the Lord. We should be present in the world not as owners but as guardians: we are responsible for the creation, not its masters. The Lord is the owner of the world.

So, with *Laudato Si'* I feel myself to have been somewhat "vindicated" (if you will excuse the term) because no other diocese in the Philippines celebrated the Feast of the Creation as we did at Imus, although many dioceses do have a service for taking care of creation. When I arrived in Manila, I "imported" that custom. So now there are two Filipino dioceses that celebrate the creation with a liturgical season!

To sum up, awareness of the creation is not simply a "green" awareness but is also a responsibility for the poor, because the earth's goods are for everyone. God wants us to be a single family enjoying the natural goods created by him. That ecological awareness or spirituality urges us toward the development of the whole person.

"Whole" is a key word in the encyclical, which was acclaimed by the cultural world at the global level. But perhaps enough attention was not paid to some passages of the encyclical that we could define, journalistically, as "politically incorrect." In them Pope Francis defends all life, including the life of the embryo; he denounces abortion, euthanasia. Often with Francis (but this also happened with other popes) we see a "value contest"—rather like a football match. When Bergoglio supports positions that please the progressive world, the Argentine pope is applauded, but when he defends more traditional values, the conservative side regards him as one of "theirs." What to do?

I'll also answer this with an example. When Pope Francis came to the Philippines, after his speeches, in the evening or at various meetings, the Filipino journalists asked me, "But is Pope Francis a conservative or a liberal?" And I replied, "He is what he is." And they repeated, "But is he a conservative or a liberal?" And I said again, "He is what he is." They couldn't understand it. It's not possible to understand Pope Francis by these categories. And indeed, I saw and remember the examples you gave. In my view this is a mistaken method. For when you consider a certain person by trying to label them you can't succeed in understanding them properly. With this way of thinking you don't really listen to the other person, who sees things from his or her own viewpoint. The label excludes their complexity. If someone, an observer, a journalist, is really honest, he finds the position that identifies a person by a label inconsistent. Someone using a label is pursuing a certain end but not the truth. Truth suffers; the church suffers when truth ends up being labeled. The ability to listen to others, to see other people's values, to find the truth in the views of other people: all that makes the labeling system collapse. For me it is fundamental to respect the mystery of the other person and of life, which is worth much more than any label.

However, the question refers to a normal fact. Or rather, the pope states the truth there where it is. Truth is not the property of a single group. When difference of culture, religion, or traditions is reduced to a label, we fail. Just as we do when we say we can only find the truth within the vision of a single group.

Returning to the encyclical Laudato Si': *why must a Christian be concerned about the environment and take care of it?*

Every Sunday we confess, "I believe in God, the Father almighty, maker of heaven and Earth." This is not just a formula or a formality: it's a matter of faith. We have a loving God who goes out of himself and unselfishly brings about the creation. Creatures are not mere objects but speak of the Trinitarian God who is love. So the attitude of looking after creatures responsibly is not just pragmatic or functional but an act of faith as Christians.

Besides, with Christ the world became the home of God incarnate. By his presence in the world Jesus Christ added even more positive value to creation, which was already "good." According to the Letter to the Hebrews, the human condition, sin, and every earthly thing are touched by the presence of God incarnate. And the Holy Spirit, who is the love and the power of God, renews the Earth and human life. It is not just an economic-environmental question. Ecology is not just a matter of the beauty or ugliness of the landscape, but above all a matter praising the Lord and sharing in God's creative activity.

But today, we are living in a throwaway culture, not sharing. Or rather, call it a culture of accumulation, hubris, and pride. I am not concerned about what I need but about what I fancy. However, we must remember that this world is not our private property. We are merely responsible for it to God and to others. We must work and take care of it in a creative way but without turning money into a new idol. We must look after the world we live in.

For some time you have been president of Caritas Internationalis, the body that oversees all the national Caritas operations and coordinates at the international level the church's effort to deal with poverty in various situations. Why did you accept this job?

According to my information, it was Caritas Asia who put forward my name as successor to Cardinal Maradiaga, who was president for the last eight years. Before him, all the other presidents were from churches in Europe. Perhaps the management committee thought the time had come for leadership from Asia. Also because over the last decade Asia has been where a series of natural disasters have struck, as well as ongoing wars and ethnic conflicts (we are thinking of the Middle East). Caritas has always been very involved in Asia—think only of the various earthquakes and tsunamis of recent years. And as bishop of Imus and archbishop of Manila, I have always been involved with Caritas. For example, I was "unofficially" in charge of managing the typhoon Hayan emergency in the metropolitan area of Manila, co-ordinating the various aid projects with Caritas Philippines, Caritas Manila, and other humanitarian organizations. Some dioceses in different parts of the world asked the Archdiocese of Manila to be the channel for their donations and assistance to areas struck by the typhoon. Perhaps they had noticed a certain capacity to get things done! Then when I heard that I was a candidate, I asked for my name to be withdrawn from the list. They answered, it's only the first stage; it does not mean that you will be the one chosen. But . . .

We know how it went. Again, why as archbishop of a "peripheral" city like Manila, a long way from Rome, did you decide to take on the burden of also becoming president of Caritas?

It's a job I do gladly, because it allows me to integrate theology and pastoral work. At the last general assembly of Caritas (May 2015), the strategic aims voted through in the assembly for the next five years showed the desire, on the part of the various Caritas operations, to bring their charitable work closer to theology and spirituality; in other words, educating hearts. Caritas volunteers must not work in a coldly ascetic way, but their hearts must be formed by the gospel. As I was also elected as president of the International Biblical Federation, I asked the Federation to help Caritas with the biblical education of its volunteers and members.

For me these two tasks to which I have been appointed are a personal enrichment and an enrichment of my work as a pastor of souls. For example, in October 2015, I was in Greece to see on the spot the work of Caritas with the refugees from the Middle East. Without my job with Caritas Internationalis I would not have had the motive or opportunity to make such a visit. There I not only saw the work of Caritas Greece and Caritas Internationalis, but I also got to know for myself the phenomenon of migration to Europe—a phenomenon that we need to study better and link more creatively with theology, because we are called to act as pastors of charity.

At least in the West—we are thinking in particular of Italy and Germany—today Caritas is synonymous with welcoming immigrant refugees. How do we, as church and as a society, behave in the face of this situation?

It is certainly a complex question, which I would like to address with three points. I have not yet gone into the matter as deeply as I would like to. For example, beginning with *Laudato Si'* and the spirituality of caring we referred to earlier: are migrants and citizens owners of their countries? They are only guardians not masters. We are all migrants. God alone gives human beings a home. We are all in transit. In Greece I asked a woman who was running the reception co-ordination, Why are you working as a volunteer? And she said, "My ancestors were refugees in Greece. I have the DNA of my refugee ancestors in my blood. My heart beats with theirs." The memory of her ancestors opened her heart. In every refugee she sees her brother, her sister, her grandfather, and grandmother.

Second, we must stress that there is legal migration but also forced migration. The refugees are forced to migrate. Every government certainly has the right to protect its own people and its own territory. But another question arises for me, to which for the moment I have no answer: why is there forced emigration, a very humiliating thing for anyone experiencing it? If there was the chance of a stable and positive life for each in their own country, would there still be this forced migration? And why is there no process to make emigration legal? Forced migration inevitably gives rise to illegal acts, for example, human trafficking and even human smuggling. Often migrants have to pay someone to take them from one place to another, and they need to spend a lot of money: these illegal movements have a very high price, and often even lead to people's deaths. Many have left their lands, their homes; they have sold their properties to pay to travel to the West. Couldn't this money be used in a legal migration process instead of ending up in the smugglers' pockets?

And the third point?

The emigration we are witnessing needs a firm decision from the international community. Violence, poverty, and destitution are the reasons that force people to leave their countries. We should remember that there are very few people who really want to leave their native land. Most people want to stay and live where they were born. In Greece I spoke to some refugees with children, and the parents' answer was always the same: we fled because of them, for our children's sake, for their future, because we want them to grow up in an environment without hatred or violence. So it is necessary for heads of government to keep on trying to ensure there is peace and calm in their own countries if they do not want to have to face the problems and difficulties of migration. Let us offer the people of every country a life of dignity.

"The poor you always have with you," Jesus says in the Gospel of John. Perhaps the church's charitable activity, including that through Caritas, may be branded as excessive "welfarism" or "benefit culture" toward the poor who will just "take advantage of it."

Perhaps people who talk like that do not have a clear idea of what Caritas does. Let's take, for example, the emergencies linked to typhoons, earthquakes, tsunamis: we have to respond with immediate aid to the victims of such natural disasters. But not all the poor want to live on welfare "benefits." Most poor people have their own dignity. They want to find work. So, according to me, it is unjust to say that humanitarian aid, this immediate "first aid," gives rise to "welfarism" or a "benefit culture." When they get the chance to stand on their own feet, poor people do so.

Moreover, most of the activity of Caritas Internationalis is not so much linked to emergency, as to poor people's whole development, because we try to give them and their communities the chance of a sustainable development. I am thinking, for example, of the work co-operatives for unemployed, exploited and marginalized women, or the training of future peasants and farmers. In Asia this work carried out by Caritas is very strong in agriculture, and education, offering scholarships for young people from disadvantaged families. In fact this is not "welfarism," because this assistance has laid down guidelines for encouraging the poor to take responsibility for their own lives.

Lastly, another activity of Caritas is what in English is called *advocacy*. In particularly difficult situations, in the face of unjust economic-social structures, or inhuman laws that do not promote the good of the poor, in order to offer long-term help, Caritas defends the rights of the poor. For example, after Pope Francis' speech to the United Nations, I was invited as president of Caritas to speak, at an event organized by the Holy See, to several dozen representatives from various countries on the social repercussions of the encyclical Laudato Si', and how it links the cry of the Earth with the cry of the poor.

Another common criticism, at least in the West, is that the church does speak about the poor but is not poor itself. It remains rich and powerful, has many possessions, and thereby puts pressure on politics. Pope Francis has repeatedly stressed his dream of a poor church for the poor. How can that project be realized in practice?

Poverty is a vocation for the church. She is called to be poor and to live among the poor. We must recognize that the church's wealth today is the result of history. The church's goods are not just spiritual monuments but also have historical and cultural value. They also witness to what a good custodian of them the church has been. As archbishop of Manila, I did not build a cathedral; I inherited a cathedral from four hundred years ago and am the custodian of it. The same goes for schools and universities. Often there is an impression of wealth, but really this wealth is the church's cultural and spiritual heritage.

But we must also ask ourselves: why is the church rich (or said to be rich) or why does it have material resources? Answer: Because the faithful give to the church to contribute to its mission. Nevertheless, that does not make parishes rich. Communities depend every Sunday on their parishioners, and in most of the world—think of Africa but also Asia and Latin America—the local churches receive help from churches in rich Western countries like the United States and Germany.

However, I have to admit that the temptation toward wealth and power is still there in the church. Hence the pope's words were much quoted and remain in force. All the church's people must be attentive and vigilant in this matter, asking forgiveness if the goods given to them to administer are not well used and restoring as much as necessary when there has been fraud. The church must continually embrace the poverty taught by the gospel.

In Conclusion

At the end of this book we would like to ask you some very simple and direct questions, so as to know you even better.

All right, let's talk!

Why are you a Christian?

Because I love Jesus.

In a word, who is Jesus for you?

Love.

Why are you a Catholic?

Because the Catholic Church offers me fullness of life and community in God who is Trinitarian love.

But the Catholic Church, throughout the centuries (and also today), has often betrayed Christ's message...

I am sad and dismayed by the fact that the church has not always been faithful to Christ's message, but God remains faithful to us and the world, even through instruments who are sinners. For me that's what really matters.

What is your episcopal motto?

Dominus est! It is the Lord! These are the words that the beloved disciple says to Simon Peter after the miraculous draft of fish. I chose that motto to remind me that it is more important to be a loving disciple than an ordained minister. Love will make me see the Lord. Love will make me a missionary to lead others to the Lord. Love will do this and not an ambitious position.

What would you change in yourself?

I'd like to have more patience; yes, be more patient. Because it would mean that I love more.

On the positive side, what aspect of your character helps you do your job?

I don't take myself too seriously. Certainly, I sometimes feel unhappy with myself. But I know I am not the savior. Jesus has already saved the world. That's the reason I can smile and laugh, even when I don't always do what I would like to or should.

Have you any hobbies?

I enjoy reading. I like detective stories, Sherlock Homes, Agatha Christie, also historical novels, for example, about

Afghanistan and Pakistan. I very much liked Khaled Hosseini's book *The Kite Runner*.[1] I also enjoy listening to music, especially classical music. Mozart fascinates me. I also enjoy listening to contemporary music and pop. I have often joined priests and parish choirs for benefit concerts. For example, on December 12, 2015, I joined with various artists for a concert dedicated to mercy and compassion to collect funds for the health needs of the poor.

You travel a lot. What does that experience mean for you?

I like watching people in the street when I am in a car or walking. I like to watch what other people are doing. As a bishop and cardinal, and now as president of Caritas Internationalis and the Catholic Biblical Federation, I have visited many countries. My horizon is broadened when I see the diversity of human cultures, the traditions, religions, languages, even the food. I feel a bit frustrated because I can't absorb everything I see, feel, and taste. But there's one thing that really satisfies me: I learn a lot from simple people who have faced various trials but have kept their dignity and their faith. Traveling makes me humble because I see people who are more gifted, who love more, and are worthier than I am.

---

1. Kahled Hosseini, *The Kite Runner* (New York: Riverhead Books, 2003).

Did you or do you practice any sport?

No, mine is not a sports family. But I like watching different sports on TV: tennis, basketball (like every Filipino), American football, volleyball, and golf. When I was younger I used to ride a bicycle, but now I just walk.

Do you cook?

When I was studying in the United States, yes. I find cooking restful. Now I don't have the chance; I am always busy! I like cooking Filipino food, *adobo*, that is chicken and pork, or *pancit*, Filipino pasta. When I was a volunteer in the Reception House of the Missionaries of Charity in Washington, I used to cook lunch for sixty people. On a number of occasions I cooked on television to teach people how to cook nourishing and inexpensive dishes for family lunch on occasions like Christmas. While I was cooking I was being interviewed or I interviewed the guests.

If you had to save one book from your library, what would you choose?

Perhaps the *Spiritual Exercises of St. Ignatius Loyola.* It is not a theological treatise, but it offers theological and pastoral lessons as a wise guide, useful for anyone with the job of guiding others.

Does your soul have a "home"?

Those moments of light and love that come unexpectedly and rapidly vanish. It seems that the soul finds its home at those moments, in those few seconds.

Which passage of the Bible is your favorite?

The appearances of the Risen Lord.

Which biblical character do you identify most closely with?

The Roman centurion standing by the cross of Jesus.

Who is your favorite saint?

St. Joseph.

You travel the world and have contacts with many people. Who is the person that has made the greatest impression on you?

I have met many people who have impressed me. If I think of recently, I met a young Syrian refugee in the refugee camp in Idomeni in Greece. He was alone. I asked him, Where are your parents? They had told him to flee even without them. For me that boy was a reminder of everything that is wrong about every war in the world. But he was also a clear signal of the strength of the human spirit. When I think about that boy, whose name I did not know, I pray for him and his parents, with a particular prayer that they may meet each other again.

Have you ever had a crisis of faith?

It may seem strange that my crisis of faith was caused by the faithfulness of God's love. I can't believe that such a love exists, that God can love the least lovable person in the world. But this love exists, as the history of the world and humanity shows. Seeing this incredible love, I believe in God.

Any regrets?

Not having learned Chinese or any other language.

Any dream you would like fulfilled?

That there might not be any more inhuman and dehumanizing poverty.

What sin do you consider to be the most serious?

Idolatry. Because instead of worshiping the true God we worship false gods. And for these idols we sacrifice human lives and the integrity of creation.

Do you think about death?

Yes, particularly when I feel weak and when I realize that my mental, psychic, and emotional capacities are not as strong as they once were. Death is saying "goodbye," letting go, but also expectant hope for those many who want to embrace and welcome us.

How do you imagine the beyond?

A banquet! A banquet where everybody, especially the world's poor, will have enough, not just of material food but also God's justice.